MW01128045

REAL HAPPY

Jesus' Suprising Path to Genuine Joy

Mike Hayes and
Dr. Jeffrey Garner

WestBow Press books may be ordered through booksellers or by contacting:

WestBow Press
A Division of Thomas Nelson & Zondervan
1663 Liberty Drive
Bloomington, IN 47403
www.westbowpress.com
844-714-3454

Author photos: Jenn Buxton, Gold Rose Studio
Cover and dust jacket design: Aaron Robertson
Editor: Yoshika Green (on amazon tag her at https://www.amazon.com/author/yoshikagreen
Editor: Ardyn Tennyson
Editor: Deborah Azzolini-Garner

ISBN: 979-8-3850-1096-7 (sc)
ISBN: 979-8-3850-1097-4 (hc)
ISBN: 979-8-3850-1098-1 (e)

Library of Congress Control Number: 2023920672

Print information available on the last page.

WestBow Press rev. date: 01/08/2024

CONTENTS

PART III: ADVANCED

ABOUT THE COVER

I hope the name chosen for this book becomes obvious as you follow the path it reveals. My desire is that you are REAL HAPPY. Real as in genuine, authentic, and thorough.

The red poppy is not only included because it looks happy, but because its story is part of this book and deserves to be told.

In 2018, I taught on The Beatitudes overlooking Galilee in northern Israel. Our tour group spread out in a semicircle with opened Bibles and journals. We were all mesmerized by the red poppies playing a game of charades all along the hillside. Their ancestors, a few centuries prior, hosted Jesus as he taught his followers, and now they spread out the red carpet for us as we reimagined his words.

When I finished the teaching that day, many of us were moved to tears by Jesus' sermon. The gentle breeze, bouncing poppies, and a placid lake in the distance pulled Jesus' sermon off the pages and into the sunlit scenery. Inspired, I suggested that we all pick a poppy and place it between the pages of our Bibles to memorialize our experience.

Back home as I reflected on the little poppy, I learned that the translation, "consider the lilies ..." in Jesus' sermon that day was a mistranslation of the word *krinon,* which is the red poppies. One might suppose that a flower is still a flower, but experiencing the blazing beauty of a thousand red poppies brings Jesus' words to life in full color, "Why are you anxious? Consider the red poppies of the field . . . they don't toil, but God clothes them in beauty."

Jesus took his text from the poppies, and their voice to us that day is a reminder that fills me with joy every time I see their bright red faces. We will touch on their significance later, but I wanted to share the intentionality behind the cover.

Mike Hayes

HAPPINESS DEFINED

We must needs confess that God is happiness itself.

—Boethius

In Real Happy, we have undertaken the task of recapturing the classic meaning of happiness, how Socrates and Saint Augustine, and ultimately Jesus, defined happiness. We realize we could have used words like joyous, wholehearted, flourishing, or even blessed. But we felt that good ol' "happy" deserved a second chance despite the prosaic smiley-faced emojis it brings to mind.

So, why happy? Well, the word happy is, simply that, happy. There is a sacred playfulness and enjoyment that happy conveys that other words just don't get—but that's not our only reason.

Most people associate Jesus with a more sublime and serious demeanor, but they don't think happy. The more we researched, the more convinced we became of Jesus' happiness. Not that it was all there was to him, but we just couldn't get away from the fact that Jesus values happiness and was himself a happy person. We became convinced that happy was a word worth redeeming because it's something we see Jesus redeeming.

The book is divided into three sections—beginner, intermediate, advanced—to indicate the graduating nature of the happy climb. Each successive Beatitude has varying levels of difficulty. This means it becomes more challenging to integrate but more rewarding to our sense of joy. The section headings mark our accomplishments and our next phase.

Beginning with chapter four, you will see a monochrome image of the poppy from the cover. We will use it's petals to convey the spectrum of happy-emotions we experienced with each Beatitude. We are convinced that happiness has a spectrum of emotions, and each happy attitude emotes a different feeling of joy. A fully bloomed happy life will feel everything from calming peacefulness to wild ecstasy. By the end of the book, our hope is that happiness will not only mean something different, but will also feel different.

Each chapter ends with a Happy Declaration. We have prayerfully created these spiritual statements as affirmations and blessings over your life. We think they help in synthesizing the chapter, but more importantly lodging the truths of it into the soil of your hearts.

Finally, Jesus' teaching through the eight Beatitudes is a happy path, a journey meant to bring you into the presence of God who is "happiness itself."

JEFFREY'S PROLOGUE

WHY WE SO HAPPY?

Man wishes to be happy,
and only wishes to be happy,
and cannot wish not to be so.
But how will he set about it?

—Blaise Pascal

In 2010, the San Francisco Giants were in the World Series with the Texas Rangers. Game One was tense for us Giants' fans. We had waited for over half a century, longing for a title. We headed into the series as big-time underdogs. The city, plastered in orange and black, belted out "Don't Stop Believing." I was parked near the Filmore, waiting for my son to finish practice at Kimball Park. Eager to catch the game, I tuned into KNBR, the Giants flagship station, and cranked up the volume.

The early Autumn evening faded into a warm orange hue. An unhoused middle-aged man dozed under a large Coast Coral tree with his grocery cart parked alongside. Steiner Street was quiet except for the distant sound of coaches' whistles and kids playing. I stared blankly at the radio when Duane Kuiper yelled, "He hits it high. He hits it deep. It! Is! Out of here!" Juan Uribe, the Giants' third baseman, had just crushed a three-run homer.

I jumped out of my car, threw back my head, and yelled, "Woohoo!"

Caught up in the excitement, I began a victory trot around my Jetta like it was a baseball diamond. As I rounded the tail of my bumper, I was met by the now awakened sleepy friend. He was jumping up and down and throwing high-fives at me.

Before I knew it, we were both hootin' and hollerin' and pump'n our fists in the air.

After several seconds of joyous reveling, I turned to crawl back in my car.

"Hey" he asked, "why we so happy?"

"What?" I replied.

"Why we so happy?" he asked again with a smile as wide as the Golden Gate Bridge.

In that moment, with that question, my fellow celebrant taught me three things about us humans.

First, we all want to be happy. The dozing man saw me celebrating and naturally jumped into celebration. I suspect this longing for happiness isn't cultural but spiritual. Smiles and laughter mean the same thing on the face of a Kenyan, Samoan or Norwegian, the unhoused and homed. From giggling toddlers to smiling elders and everywhere in between, our souls long for happiness. We seek out happy moments.

Second, we all want to share our happiness. It's no fun celebrating alone. Had someone not joined me, my one-man party would have been short-lived, and my joyful jog around the car would have quickly become an awkward half-trot. Thankfully, my new buddy validated my feelings and amplified my rejoicing. Though we didn't know each other, we understood each other.

Third, we want our happiness to last. While my newfound friend was happy to celebrate with me, he wanted to understand the meaning behind the moment. Quite honestly, his question endeared me to him. When he asked, "Why we so happy?" he was saying, "This happiness will last longer if I know what it's all about." I think that is what Jesus offers us; he comes along and offers us a happiness that is meaningful, lasting and spiritual.

I frequently think about the joyful courage of my jubilant San Franciscan, bravely trotting the imaginary bases with me. If the pages that follow inspire you to jump around the car with us, I will be happier than I was with the Giants' 2010 World Series.

San Francisco
January 2023

P.S. *Thank you, Mike, for the gift of your confidence in me. The gracious invitation to share in the articulation of your encounter with happiness on the Mount of Beatitudes was a gift only surpassed by the fun we've had working together on this Happy Project. You are one of the most generous humans I've ever met, living out an Abrahamic way of blessing others.*

MIKE'S PROLOGUE

HOW I MISSED HAPPINESS

He who has God is real happy.[1]

— Saint Augustine

My junior high gym was typical of the sixties, with creaky wooden-slatted floors and ragged basketball nets. The walls of our gym echoed with fifty years of laughter and sweaty kids in baggy shorts running back and forth under the dim, dusty lights. I wanted to excel in that gym, to measure up. Our gym coach was an old warhorse, his deep wrinkles and thinning hair testified to his years of toiling with hormone-fevered adolescents. I wanted to impress him. I was a fair athlete for my age, but I had a problem. It wasn't with the gym or the coach, the other kids, or even with me. My problem was God, or at least the one represented by my church.

During my high school years, I began to develop real consternation about my church. Specifically, the rules it imposed. I was raised in a Pentecostal church, and what I've learned in later years is every church has its own rules, its own ways, and its own culture. From Baptist to Catholic, they all have their own brand of difficult rules, and they all do their own kind of good.

Our church had something called "standards of holiness" which included modest dress. For me, that meant I was not allowed to wear gym shorts in PE, hence my consternation. This is what I remember about our gym shorts. They were navy blue and always wrinkled because fourteen-year-olds make a habit of stuffing their gym shorts in their locker, don't take them home for weeks, and sweat in them every day in gym class. Even with an elastic waistband and the oversized leg holes that fell to my knees, my church thought they were too immodest! At fourteen, I loved my dad and God, wanted to please both, and disappoint neither. For some reason, I also wanted to be thought of as holy at my church, so I didn't wear the gym shorts. To worsen matters, I had to take a note from the pastor that excused me from "dressing out" as my coach called it.

In those days, there was no such thing as politically correct verbiage, and the coaches could pretty much say anything they wanted. One day, the coach announced, "boys, it's raining outside so we're gonna stay indoors and play dodgeball." We filed into a picking line. As the team captains chose sides, I stood there in my blue jeans while everyone was dressed out in their sweaty, wrinkled, oversized gym shorts. The whole scene must have perturbed my coach because he looked at me and said, "Hey, you! Mike! The loser that can't wear gym shorts! Sit over there against the wall. If you can't wear gym shorts, you can't play."

Sadly, that moment was typical of many that came before and after it in my very religious childhood. Downcast, I walked to the bleachers to watch all the boys in shorts play ball. Watching my classmates play dodgeball while sitting in my jeans, I felt shame that turned into frustration, and then anger. I sat for several minutes in those feelings until it dawned on me that I didn't know what or who I was angry at. Was I angry with God? Not really because the only thing I knew about God was Jesus and I liked Jesus. I just didn't think Jesus would be so uncool as to not let me wear my gym shorts. Was I angry with my dad? No, he didn't come up with the holiness standards. In a desperate need to have my anger land, I chose to put it squarely on the church. To me, the church had a long index finger and pointed nose. The unreasonable rules and rule-enforcers made me unhappy.

I didn't know it then, but I was facing a dilemma that millions around the world find themselves in. I really loved Jesus but was unhappy and at times even fearful in the church. I meet people almost every day that have some kind of "church hurt" similar to mine, where the prohibitions may be different, but the hurt similar. One thing I know about hurt, big or small, church hurt or otherwise, it's hard to see God as happy or wanting us to be happy when we are hurt.

We don't have to be dealing with hurt to have a difficult relationship with happiness either. Some just feel undeserving of happiness, while others feel stuck with an unhappy personality. Whatever the reason for our love-hate relationship with happiness, the absurd thing is most Americans are unhappy most the time. After all, this is the "Age of Anxiety."

The subject of happiness is not one I would have ever spoken about, let alone write about had it not been for an experience with it on the Mount of Beatitudes. I returned home from the red poppy hill moment eager to uncover what happened to me and those present with me. For eight weeks following, I taught on happiness, the kind that Jesus offered. As I researched, I wondered how in thirty years of pastoring I had missed the idea that beatitude meant happy or blissful. *If I had missed this what else had I missed?*

Although the idea to write about my beatitude discoveries was mine, I felt that it would be truer to the spirit of the happy attitudes to do this with a friend, so I asked Jeffrey to write with me. We aren't experts in the science of happiness, but we are serious students of Jesus and his teachings on the subject, and we are eager to share our findings with you.

In the first two chapters we work through three questions. Where did Jesus get his theology on happiness? What was the socio-political setting of these happy talks? What does this mean for people today?

As previously mentioned, chapters three through ten are each dedicated to a single happy attitude. We note its counter-cultural nature and significance, the emotional range of the happy attitude, and most importantly the Good News of how to engage in its joy.

Chapter eleven offers a bonus beatitude, a *makarism,* tucked away for the times when we are offended, disappointed, and confused.

A final word here on the flow: we wanted *Real Happy* to have academic integrity but be written in the voice of an ordinary conversation. Jeffrey and I open each chapter with personal stories set off by our name and a different font. The body of the chapters will then read in first person plural to reflect our co-authorship.

I hope this book is a tool that leads you into an experience of the kind of happiness Jesus wants for you. I pray that your happiness will be blissfully contagious to your world. May you experience, as I continue to do, that Jesus' words, then and now, are uniquely transforming, currently relevant, and that He is absolutely interested in your happiness.

Dallas
January 2023

HAPPINESS
A BRIEF HISTORY

Happiness is no laughing matter.
—Richard Whatley

Early Greek philosophers thought that Tyche, the goddess of fortune, only shared happiness with a few handpicked mortals. Luck, according to their thinking, was the only way to be happy. In fact, the word happy and happened both parlay this Greek notion into the Old English word *hap,* meaning chance or lucky.

Socrates (470-399 BCE) was the first philosopher to challenge these popular assumptions on happiness. Happiness, he argued, should not be understood as mere luck; it was something for people to *pursue*. He was the first to urge the best Greek minds to acknowledge and pursue happiness. His conceptual challenge on happiness pushed earlier philosophical discussions to the margins and gave philosophy a new mission: "Since we all desire happiness, how can we be happy? —that is the next question!"[2] The question, forced on Socrates critics, created a longing and an answer to the human quest. His philosophical agenda swept through the Grecian world, and gained many adherents and famous students.

Plato (428-348 BCE), like his teacher Socrates, reasoned happiness was within our power to grasp, however, few ever approached the kind of virtue and wisdom necessary to achieve happiness. Plato believed Socrates "alone approached the goal of 'becoming like a god,' of being truly happy."[3] Plato saw happiness in spiritual and other worldly terms, a god-like quest.

Aristotle (384-322 BCE), Alexander the Great's tutor, elaborated on Plato's theory by philosophizing that all things exist for a purpose—and humanity's purpose was to be happy.

Using words like *makarios* (happy), and *eudaemonia* (good spirit), he described happiness as "the good life," by which he meant not simply virtuous, but the exercise of ten virtues.

By the time of Aristotle's death, the Study of Happiness was the undisputed goal of every philosophical sect in Greece. Philosophers believed happiness to be humanity's ultimate desire and the final ending to which our purpose reaches; and unlike the preclassical world, each human being, not the gods, was responsible for his own happiness.

By the turn of the first century, happiness was all the trendy rage in the Mediterranean world. The four great schools of Athens and their Roman successors kept the pursuit of happiness happy alive but still out of reach for the common folk. In a world where slavery was normative, women were property, and education was for the privileged few, the vast majority of people were unworthy of happiness, and this went unchallenged in the West for centuries.

This book is about one teacher who changed all of that. How from a nameless hillside, he redefined and redistributed happiness, and how his path and words take all of us on a journey from unlucky to happy.

PART I

BEGINNER

CHAPTER 1

JESUS' TED TALK

A Happy Idea Worth Spreading

> *If you know these things, happy are you if you do them.*
>
> –Jesus of Nazareth

In the opening sequence of the black and white film *Stardust Memories,* fifteen to twenty people sit in a train car awaiting their departure.

The glum Sandy Bates surveys his fellow passengers—a yawning toothless woman, a cynical academic in round Windsor glasses, a stodgy retiree occupying two seats. Down the row from Sandy, a whimpering man wipes his nose on his shirt sleeve. Sandy's eyes shift to the young professional sitting across from him, who returns his glance with a what-are-you-looking-at glare. Behind Sandy, two middle-aged sourpusses glower with soulless gazes. The economy car is cursed with bored, vacant-eyed and miserable passengers.

Tick-tick-tick, tick-tick-tick, the train clocks belabor the gloomy atmosphere.

Glimpsing out his window, Sandy spies a private, first-class train car on a parallel track, also awaiting its departure, but heading in the opposite direction.

Inside, important men and beautiful women laugh, toast

champagne, and enjoy the life of privilege. A flirty socialite giggles at him and blows a kiss his way. The passengers gleefully chat and backslap. Sandy despairs. He glances around once more, drawing comparisons between the two cars; the clocks seem to tick faster and louder. Why isn't he in the sparkling car with sparkling people? Then his train lurches to a start. A look of panic comes over his face. He jumps up and frantically scrambles for the exit. Too late. Sandy realizes he is stuck in the lifeless bore, banished to the economy class, and exiled from the first-class happy car.

The scene and ticking clocks together describe the kind of anxiety we have about happiness. When we look around at our dull or hapless life, we feel time is running out on any hope of a happy life. We spy another family laughing at a restaurant while our kids cry and complain, or we observe a couple holding hands walking down the street, noting we have not yet found a soul mate. *Tick, tick, tick, tick*. . . . We frantically look around at our dull, worn economy seats and think, if only I were talented, gregarious, or came from a family of privilege, then I would be in the happy private train.

The *loco*motion drags our unlucky life in a direction we do not want to go but feel powerless to stop.

If Jesus Gave a TED Talk

These days, most people would see God and happiness in separate train cars. We tend to think that God is more about holiness, justice, or compassion and that happiness is an unrelated extra, a frill. But did you know that the Bible speaks directly about happiness? And no, it's not tucked away in some cryptic, hidden passage. Happiness is front and center and makes up Jesus' "big idea worth spreading," which today we might liken to a TED Talk.

Jesus debuted his happy message in what we know more commonly as the Beatitudes.[4] To emphasize his big idea, Jesus chose the Greek word, *makarios,* which we translate as "blessed." Makarios even sounds like bobbing cheerios. In a simple and straightforward translation, the word means "happy."[5]

The Greek word originated to describe the worry-free, high life of the Greek gods. By the time of Jesus, *makarios* had become a pop culture reference for the one-percenters who were happy because they didn't struggle or worry like the impoverished and working class. In effect, Jesus seized a word monopolized by the gods, the wealthy moguls, and landowners and redistributed it to common folk.

Of all the topics one might have expected from his first public discourse, religion topping the list, Jesus' big idea worth spreading was an idea on happiness. Here is how the farmers, bakeshop owners, peasants, homemakers, servants, fishermen, seamstresses, and students heard it that day (Matthew 5:3-11)

> Happy are the poor in spirit...
> Happy are those who mourn...
> Happy are the meek ...
> Happy are those who hunger and thirst for justice...
> Happy are the merciful...
> Happy are the pure in heart...
> Happy are the peacemakers...
> Happy are those who are persecuted for righteousness...
> Happy are you when others revile you and utter falsehoods against you...
> Rejoice and be glad...

Makarios rang as a surprising word choice to a crowd mainly comprised of working-class Galileans (today's northern Israel) living under Roman occupation. National oppression, religio-political corruption, human trafficking, censored speech and monitored public behavior darkened day-to-day life for Galileans. Extreme economic inequality plus the weight of Roman taxes created unfavorable living conditions such as physical sickness, poor mental health, poverty, and homelessness. In short, the average person was desperate, depressed, and hoping for a revolution or liberator to rally the public and overthrow the false narrative of Rome's peace propaganda.

In this tenuous and sensitive social climate, Jesus makes the risky decision to launch his public debut on happiness. Delivered in poetic pentameter and set off with the phrase, "Happy are the...," he holds the gaze of a people hungry for justice, fairness, and relief from oppression with a talk on happiness. Then, in another risky choice, he upsets the stigma of all that we typically associate with cursedness and unhappiness— poverty, hunger, oppression, sadness, and powerlessness—by using those very words to describe happiness and joy. He proclaims a new truth; your external status cannot take hostage your internal happiness.

Reimagine the *Stardust Memories* scene. You sit in the hapless economy train car, but this time instead of wanting to flee to the first-class car for happiness, imagine something happening in you, in the same seat, with the same people. A no-strings-attached joy pops and fizzles wildly within. You are the happiness the world wants to know, not a train car. You are no longer comparing your insides to other people's outsides. Instead, you possess laughter in your soul, gratefulness for this gift of joy, and eagerness to share it with your traveling companions. Eagerly, you look around for any opportunity to be an agent of this serendipity; you embrace your joy as a calling to be an undercover agent of the Heavenly City that Smiles.

Jesus was all about showing us that the happy life, or what he called "the abundant life," was available no matter what train car we find ourselves in.[6] In one happy attitude after another, and in the most unconventional of ways, Jesus teaches us how near and real happiness is to all of us.

❖ My Happy Declaration

Today, at the beginning of this journey, I choose to believe and declare that God WANTS me to be happy! My desire for happiness is not trivial or unimportant to God, but is the focus of God's love for me.

➢ Up Next

Isn't it true that anticipating a trip, the planning, packing, and research are just as joyful as the journey? Before we journey into the first happy attitude (Chapter 4), we encourage you to prepare with us in the next chapter. We will answer questions like, was Jesus happy, and if so, why was he happy? Does the community have anything to do with happiness, or is it just a matter of being personally responsible for one's happiness? How do we orient ourselves toward the happy climb?

CHAPTER 2

THE CITY THAT SMILES

Jesus' Merry Band Of Followers

I dream'd in a dream, I saw a city invincible to the attacks of the whole of the rest of the earth;
I dream'd that was the new City of Friends;
Nothing was greater there than the quality of robust love—it led the rest;
It was seen every hour in the actions of the men of that city,
And in all their looks and words.

—Walt Whitman

Jeffrey: Every author has a writing process. I am blessed to pastor a small, neighborhood church in downtown San Francisco. Our church is filled with diversity and belovedness. Because of our communal context, we are a perfect petri dish for testing content. When I told everyone about "The Real Happy Project," they were enthused to participate and intrigued at the probability of finding their stories or suggestions in the manuscript. We decided to turn The Happy Book into a teaching series so they could help craft the content. On Mondays, I disseminated the corresponding book chapter for beta reading and feedback. I opened the teaching series with the chapter you are about to read. The discussion followed very closely with the sections in this chapter, the main idea being that God is not just interested, but invested, in our happiness.

As I shared how Jesus came to form his theology of joy, Milo, one of our community members, uncharacteristically got up and walked out. I was briefly distracted, wondering if I said something offensive. Eventually, he returned, his face flushed. Afterward, Milo pulled me aside and apologized for walking out abruptly, explaining that he needed to compose himself.

Milo was raised in a hyper-religious sect that stressed fearing God and pleasing God. Leaders within his religious group used shame and fear to motivate rule-keeping and doctrinal compliance. Milo strove to please God, but felt like God wasn't happy with him. This led to an ongoing insecurity about his salvation.

Choked up and short of breath, Milo spent the next thirty minutes sharing his backstory with me. We stood there for a moment, hugging and crying together in the sacredness of his life.

Then he said to me, "All my life I strove to make God happy, today for the first time I was overcome with the truth that all my life God has wanted to make me happy!"

Lost in Translation: Blessed vs. Happy

Pick up almost any Bible today, turn to Matthew 5:3 and instead of reading the word "happy" you will read:

> Blessed are the poor in spirit...
> Blessed are those who mourn...
> Blessed are the meek...
> Blessed are those who hunger and thirst for justice...
> Blessed are the merciful...
> Blessed are the pure in heart...
> Blessed are the peacemakers...

> Blessed are those who are persecuted for righteousness...
> Blessed are you when others revile you and utter falsehoods against you...
> Rejoice and be glad...

Why did English translators choose "blessed" to translate *makarios* when there is a New Testament Greek word (*eulogetos)* dedicated to "blessed"?[7] What was lost by taking a word classically translated as happy, and spiritualizing it into "blessed"?

Translators opted for the word blessed in lieu of happy because "happy" reduces too easily into happy-go-lucky, fleeting emotion. Well-intended translators didn't want to trivialize *makarios,* so they chose a secondary word, 'blessed.' They rightly recognized that Jesus was giving us more than warm and fuzzy feelings. But by un-happifying the translation, we lose a provocative paradox that Jesus may be teeing up. Moreover, we distance ourselves from the opportunity to experience the playful and delightful gist of God's joy for his children.

Some might argue that it's foolhardy for us to make a big deal out of a word. Rather than an etymological rant on *makarios, happy, beatitude,* and *eudaemon,* let's experiment with two questions.[8]

What feeling does the word "happy" emote?

And what about the word "blessing"?

Happy splashes us with a sense of God's enjoyment of our life. Blessing, on the other hand, quiets us to receive a prayer or offer a gratitude for our meal. Both are beautiful. Both are from the same creator. But one gets no space while the other has a monopoly.

We think the time is right to rediscover happiness in the heart of Jesus.

The Miracle of Happy Hour

There is no dichotomy between the happiness of man and the designs of God.
— Abraham Joshua Heschel

Whether you are religious or irreligious, we all must confront a false narrative spun by our culture. The religious fiction says God doesn't care if you're happy, he just cares about righteousness and rules, holiness and seriousness. The irreligious fiction says He doesn't care at all.

An early Jesus story provides us with constructive feedback on the dupery of these false narratives.

John 2 recounts Jesus attending a weeklong Galilean wedding festival at a local vineyard. Three days into the celebration, the unthinkable happens—the wine runs dry. Families have journeyed more than a hundred miles to toast and laugh and celebrate. Whether it was a lack of planning or thirsty guests we aren't told, but we know the wedding coordinator is scrambling and coming up short. If the news gets out it will besmirch the bridegroom and undo the happy party.

Wine was a first century must in any celebration. In fact, Dionysus, the Greek god of merriment and mirth, was the god of wine. Though Jews did not have a god of wine, they did have One God whose story they celebrated with wine. Passover, the Jewish holiday commemorating their liberations from Egypt, involved four glasses of wine. The Sabbath and all religious festivals involved wine. Jewish observers of the Torah frequently reminded themselves "wine that cheers God and men" (Judges 9:13) should be given to "those in bitter distress" (Proverbs 31:6-7). Wine was the forerunner to laughter and joyousness, the primer and the finisher of any memorable party.

Aware of the tipping point, Jesus' mother instructs him to do his thing. At her behest, he saves the day. With nothing but ordinary water and six empty stone jars he crushes it. "Muah!" (lips kissing fingers). One hundred and eighty gallons of oak-aged purple joy is shelved and ready for pouring. This story gurgles and giggles with delight. Miraculous signs made up of wine and weddings and surprises do that. It's not just that the party goes on, but that we also catch a glimpse of God's playfulness.

Now we can think of a dozen preferable miracles to debut one's ministry. Why not heal a child? Or raise someone from the dead? Or call fire down from heaven on the Romans? Water to wine?! We are told that winemaking was "the first of the *signs* through which he revealed his glory" (John 2:11, NIV). It was a sign, not merely a miracle. John's distinction matters because a sign points to a greater truth (means to an end) whereas a miracle is a supernatural wonder (an end in itself). So what truth was this sign highlighting? Primarily it signals that Jesus is sent from God, but the choice of water-to-wine flags that God is really interested in our happiness!

Moses' first sign was turning water into blood (Exodus 7). Elijah's first sign was extinguishing water into the thin air, catalyzing a three-year drought (1 Kings 17). This story tops all the other water-miracle stories. Without it, we are left to think that God is only concerned with serious grievances and not simple happiness.

As a first miracle, happiness is revealed as a priority to God. And through Jesus, God is established as the real God of Happiness. The one-hundred and eighty splurging gallons is enough to baptize all the attendees in the Father's joy.

Fatherly Joy

Where does Jesus get this idea that God is happy or that God cares about our happiness?

Several months before his happy hillside pronouncements, a "purist" grassroots movement gathered in Galilee. A prophet named John protested the urban corruption in the wilderness, outside the cosmopolitan world of Roman politicians and Jewish religious elites. John encouraged the people to baptize in the Jordan River, a spiritual ritual expressing repentance and sorrow for the corruption. Followers of the movement longed to please God and wanted to ready themselves for His presence.

Jesus, an unknown young man from a good-for-nothing village, joined in this revival and something gloriously unexpected happened.

It's worth noting that for centuries in Jewish lore, all heavenly visions and angelic voices were preceded by a booming, "Fear not!" In other words, encounters with the Divine were usually terrifying. Anyone present for that heaven-parting-moment would have anticipated a "Fear Not" boom followed by visions of fiery chariots, stampeding horses, or angelic armies. But in a radical departure from hundreds of recorded encounters, a dove descended! Followed by these shocking and delightfully happy words,

This is my son!
I love him!
He brings me great joy!

NO ONE was expecting the joyful outburst of a proud Father.

Let's also note that Jesus had not turned water to wine or given a profound speech. He hadn't started a compassion movement; he was just one in a crowd. Yet, he hears and believes that God is a doting Father who is happy with him. In the *first* recorded entry of Jesus' experience with God, Jesus perceives himself as someone who makes God happy simply by breathing, by existing. This entire baptismal experience voices Jesus' theology of happiness.

That happiness is so deeply embedded in him, he bursts

onto his missional stage with a happy gospel. He preaches Good News, not doom and gloom. Jesus' Father was happy! From under the fluttering wings of the happy dove Jesus announces the same Good News to us. It's a joyful message he shares at parties, picnics, and over shared meals. And here is the radical truth that Jesus embodies: how we see God is how we see everything. If we see God is happy, we will see the happiness of everything.

The Happy Climb

> Now when Jesus saw the crowds,
> he went up on a mountainside
> and sat down.
> His disciples came to him,
> and he began to teach them.
>
> [insert Sermon on the Mount]
>
> When Jesus had finished saying these things,
> the crowds were amazed at his teaching.[9]

When Jesus sees the crowds, he gets away to a natural amphitheater, a sacred classroom big enough for anyone who wants to come. He doesn't give the talk from a synagogue or Temple courtyard, but on a poppy-covered hill. A frequent feature of Jesus' pedagogy is bringing the sacred into the everyday blahs. He teaches *along the way* and atop mountains, around tables, and inside of boats. He wants to connect happiness with nameless hills and everyday conversations.

Jesus' move from the crowds to the mountainside symbolizes two things: first, his words are going to be counter cultural. It's another way of saying, *you won't find Jesus' wisdom in the cultural norms and crowd think.* You'll have to get off the beaten path. Second, any climb requires effort and intention. No one will stumble into his happy oracles. Climbing mountains takes commitment. Jesus does two things incredibly well. He includes outcasts misfits, and those otherwise lacking confidence; and, secondly, he takes them with him on a climb and helps them journey to the absolute best version of themselves.

Up on the mountainside was a sociological hint to the first century readers. Mountains were places for building cities. This mountainside, as Jesus will say in a moment, is a "city set on a hill that cannot be hid" (Matthew 5:14).

The ziggurats of Mesopotamia, the pyramids of Egypt, and the Acropolis of Athens were the great city centers of their day because people wanted to be as close to the gods as earthly possible. These summits were the presumed touchpoints of heaven and earth. Ancient people therefore centered their lives around a mountain, a ziggurat, a hill, so that the divine safely guided their life.

Jesus' hike up a mountainside echoes Moses' ascent of Mount Sinai. Just as Moses ascended onto the Mount of God and initiated Israel into a covenant, so here Jesus in a familiar manner ascends the mountain and issues an edict for God's Society. The similarities echo forth—mountains, ascents, calls to heavenly citizenship, how-to instructions, and crowds that look on in utter amazement.

There are, however, subtle yet striking differences. Moses begins with Ten To-Dos and To-Don'ts. Jesus begins with Eight Happy Attitudes. Moses directs us to what humans should be doing. Jesus blesses us into being human. Moses' commands end with a warning. Jesus' blessings end with promise. Perhaps the most striking difference is Moses ascends and descends alone from the Mountain, but by the time Jesus descends a whole crowd has followed him up and back (see Matthew 7:28).

At a first glance, the mountain may seem inaccessible and exclusionary, but in truth it empowers and elevates the people to new heights. The mountain does not cull out the weak but culls out those unwilling to discover the strength they have with God.

His disciples came to him, and he began his Masterclass. In the chapter before the climb, Jesus calls four disciples—Peter, James, John, and Andrew. Discipleship was a pedagogy, a specialized method of learning. By toting along four disciples for the happy climb Jesus was underscoring that happiness is not a whimsical feeling or jovial personality but a learned attitude. As Jesus will define happiness, it's not luck or chance, but a spiritual environment, that is honed in us.

We mentioned in the previous chapter that the eight happy oracles were Jesus' big idea worth sharing. What we mean is the entire sermon in its straightforward poetic flow, can be read in fifteen minutes, and like a TED Talk it is brief, to the point, and introduces a big idea. But it departs from a TED Talk when we read "his disciples came to him and he taught them"(Matthew 5:1-2). His happy apprentices climbing the mountain to be mentored resembles a Masterclass more than a talk or even a sermon.

The difference between a TED Talk and a Masterclass are as follows:

TED Talk	**Masterclass**
Purpose: to introduce and evaluate an idea	Purpose: to internalize and master the idea
Synopsis to a crowd	Lesson to apprentices
Commitment to listen	Commitment to practice
Being informed	Being transformed

In Happiness: A Brief History, we pointed out how happiness was trending in the four major philosophical schools of the day. Each school took a slightly different approach to the subject. But just in case this gets lost on us, we want to reiterate that, happiness was a formal apprenticed study. Happiness was a craft worth learning and honing. There's a bit of a disconnect for us because our universities and schools are about making a good living, but the philosophical schools of that day were about making a happy life.

These schools operated under the premises that happiness was not a pill you took, a lucky break you got, or a privileged life into which you were born. Happiness was a practice. You apprenticed into the happy fields of Elysium, and pilgrimaged into the happy city of God.

We challenge you to commit, in whatever way that looks like for you, to the practices of Jesus masterclass on happiness. The fact that you are reading this, studying happiness, says much about your desire and drive. Our experience is most people don't see the extraordinary hope that is at work within them. That spark and spunk that God sees *in you.* If you've gotten this far, you have demonstrated enough one-word-at-a-time determination to summit the real happy hillside.

The More the Merrier. Jesus begins the tutelage with four newly initiated disciples- just four.[10] But when we finish the tutoring session three chapters later and lift up our eyes, the hillside is packed with students! Joy is contagious! Holy happiness is magical in that it seeks out the hungry and thirsty, it rewards the seeker and quester. In one afternoon, Jesus' idea had gone first century viral.

Jesus never describes his happy oracles in the singular. All eight sayings are punctuated in plural promise. If you're from the south, it would sound like this, "Y'all are happy when you're . . . ." His happy promise was a communal one Jesus invites you to join generations of happy travelers on pilgrimage, not to journey alone. The happiness he offers isn't an enlightened state an individual reaches alone on a Himalayan mountaintop, but a caravan of happy folk sharing in the joys and struggles of life, practicing together.

Jesus knows we are not merely searching for our smile, but

for a community to share our smile with. We were made for the kind of happiness that happens in community. Jesus knew this. Jesus addressed this. Jesus blessed this.

God's happiness is an expansive, contagious, and generous city. "You [all] are the light of the world. A city set on a hill cannot be hidden" (Matthew 5:14).

We found it interesting that every current study we looked at on happiness makes community and relationships ground zero in the fight for happiness.[11] This can be discouraging for those who have no community or who have experienced relational loss. Jesus, however, offers to bring the community and relationships into our path as we take personal responsibility to journey up the mountain.

For those reading this that feel lonely, we feel a special word for you. You, especially, are not excluded from Jesus' happy city. Christ's communal happiness was designed with your unique needs and lonely situations in mind. Even if you are a person who cannot get physically connected to a community in your present circumstance, you can begin right now to lock arms with a cloud of happy-attitude witnesses that goes back for more than fifty generations. Moreover, you are presently in the company of God through his Spirit. We invite you to pray this prayer:

> *Dear God, I feel alone. Would you please bring the joy of your Presence into my heart right now? And would you guide me into a community of people that live out your happy attitudes? Thank you. Amen.*

Now in return we bless you with this one:

> *Father, you see this child, alone, confined, isolated. Send them your comfort, the Presence.*

Because they cannot climb the mountain, bring to them your community in unexpected ways so they may experience the joy of being part of the city of God. Help them to feel, sense, and recognize moments of communion with you and community with your creation. Thank you for Jesus who shows us what true communal joy is like. In Jesus' name, Amen.

So far, we have seen Jesus and happiness go hand-in-hand. His first recorded experience with God centers on happiness. His first miracle is about happiness, his first teaching is about happiness, even his first proclamation is called "Good News." All our life God has pursued us with happy sunsets, awe-inspiring sky galleries, and abounding nature scapes. God has pursued all his children with new opportunities in each breath, hope in every morning, and grace to close out each day. The question now becomes how do we engage and make ourselves available for the happiness God intends for us?

❖ My Happy Declaration

Recognizing that God desires my happiness, I declare I will commence the climb that it requires to experience it. Unlike works for salvation, this climb is an exercise in an attitude adjustment. I will not be alone in my quest. I will join my fellow seekers, my community that lives in the city that smiles.

➢ Up Next:

What role does listening play in hearing Jesus' happy oracles? Aren't all happy concepts and paths leading to the same happy place? Does it really matter how I listen or how I read? In the next chapter we learn that there is a listening context in which to hear Jesus' happy message.

CHAPTER 3

EAR TO THE GROUND

Listening Our Way To Laughter

Laughter is the closest thing to the grace of God.
—Karl Barth

In 2007, renowned violinist Joshua Bell participated in an experiment organized by the Washington Post. During the morning rush, he played his ten-million-dollar Stradivarius violin in the busy L'Enfant Plaza metro station in Washington D.C. Bell, who commands top dollar for his performances, played for 45 minutes, but only a few people stopped to listen. The people who stopped likely had ears for classical music and recognized the beauty of the unconventional moment.

The study concluded that preconceived notions, expectations, and the context of the encounter often constrain a person's ability to appreciate beauty. The Joshua Bell Experiment sparked a conversation about the role of context and expectations in shaping our experiences and perceptions of art and beauty.

Happiness, like music, is beautiful and artful. It too can be shaped by our expectations and focus. The attention and intention with which we approach a happy life influence the quality of happiness we experience. For example, if we think that happiness is found in Ivy League universities or in a high

GPA, we may overlook it in the ordinary plazas of life. It's possible that happiness of a higher quality, that a different kind and unusual path exists right within earshot.

How Are We Listening?

He opened his mouth, and taught them, saying...
—Matthew 5:2

The Fourth Gospel opens with the words, "In the beginning was the Word," then calls the reader to listen, no less than fifty times. This motif of listening is the first and final mark of true students. The idea is that whatever we are hearing, we are becoming. And whatever we listen to the most, we become most like.

Just before scribing Jesus' first happy oracle, Matthew sets up Jesus' words with this clunky redundancy. Why not just say, "Jesus said"? The phrase, *anoixas edidasken legōn* or "opened, taught, saying" flags the imminent teaching as a King's Decree, and highlights the inaugural nature of the moment. The three verbs are not verbose, but technical jargon.

"Opened his mouth" reads as an edict, the language of a king, and reminds us Jesus' words are not merely editorial. "Taught them" additionally reveals Jesus as a Wisdom teacher. Jesus isn't just a king, but a wise King who teaches rather than dictates. His words flow within the stream of Jewish tradition called the Wisdom Tradition. The Jewish Wisdom teachers tutored their students into the happy path. Finally, "saying" is the equivalent of our quotation marks, indicating that what follows is a verbatim quote.[12]

Matthew would have us know that Jesus is the King of this Happy Kingdom. His words hold sway, keep court, and are timeless. The language of "opened his mouth" carries the same force as "Mr. Speaker, Mr. Vice President, Members of

Congress, my fellow Americans." Jesus' words that Spring afternoon were equivalent to our State of the Union address. And the eight happy oracles that follow set the prophetic agenda of his Kingdom. Finally, the scope of the oracles is not merely about making a select few happy but about happifying the whole world *through* the happy few.[13]

With this literary construct, Matthew calls us to attention and instructs us to consider our listening filters.

Try as we might, we all listen with a bias. For example, when U.S. citizens listen to a State of the Union Address, we all hear the same words but listen differently. Political pundits listen critically. Wall Street listens with an economic filter, while foreign correspondents listen with a global perspective. The opposing party listens suspiciously, while party faithfuls listen proudly.

How we listen is what we hear. And what we hear determines how we respond.

The sounds of joy ring all around our metro-driven lives. But the happy oracles work their miracle on happy ears. The technical term is "*kavanah*-listening."[14] *Kavanah* means we set an intention. What do we want? How open are we to spiritual serendipity? What kind of reader-listener do we want to be? How are we listening to Jesus' words? Critically? Self-righteously? Curiously? Or humbly?

We moved away from the crowds to get here and climbed through a few chapters to sit here. Now Matthew urges us to listen for the four-string Stradivarius voice of happiness as we step into the wide-open spaces of the first happy attitude.

❖ My Happy Declaration

I understand the importance of "how" I hear, which determines "what" I hear, which determines the choices I make. So, I determine to hear Jesus' joyful words with humble, happy, receptive ears.

➢ Up Next: Happy are the poor in spirit... (Matt 5:3)

Now that you have your contextual bearings, let's sequence through each happy attitude as they were spoken from the mountainside. In Chapter four, we answer three questions. Is the first happy attitude a prerequisite for the eight that follow it? How does the first happy attitude undo one of the most popular human approaches to happiness? What did Jesus mean when he said, poor in spirit?

PART II

INTERMEDIATE

Happyluah! Congratulations on completing the first leg of your happy journey. Before you jump into the Intermediate section, visit ImRealHappy.com or follow the QR code to access free supplemental resources.

CHAPTER 4

THE CLASS THAT JUDAS MISSED

Making Room For Happiness

Spaciousness

Dear God,
I am so afraid to open my clenched fists!
Who will I be when I have nothing left to hold on to?
Who will I be when I stand before you with empty hands? Please help me to gradually open my hands and to discover that I am not what I own, but what you want to give me.

— Henri J.M. Nouwen

Jeffrey: "You can find five-star meals right here!" Benedict exclaimed, pointing to the trash bin behind a Michelin-star restaurant. "And it's all free! We waste so much perfectly good stuff."

He opened the large trash bin, found a bread roll, and handed it to me with a smile.

Benedict's red bandana made him look like a pirate, but when he smiled, which was most of the time, the large, crooked smile spoiled the Captain Jack Sparrow look.

A little after midnight on a Friday evening, I traipsed behind my city-life guide in the TL (Tenderloin). We plopped down on one of his many curbs; he was unhoused and truly saw the world as his proverbial "oyster." He pulled out his guitar and picked away. In another life, he was a professional studio musician but the pressures of keeping up got to him.

"Seemed like everyone owned a piece of me, so I chose the better life, free from the demands of society." He sounded like he was trying to convince me to join him.

Benedict was a meth addict brought about by the opioid crisis. He never gave me the backstory to that.

"I've been trying to shake this addiction for a long time," he admitted.

We saw each other around the neighborhood several times a week. He was happy, easy-going, super friendly, and always looking to help a friend. One day he found a grand piano in an abandoned church half a mile away and decided to bring it to Lighthouse as a gift. I saw him pushing the piano up Van Ness, Highway 101, which runs through the gut of San Francisco. Cars honked, and drivers cursed. Benedict didn't care or even notice. He found a piano and didn't want it to go to waste.

During the pandemic, I lost track of Benedict. I didn't see him around anymore and wondered what became of him. I worried that his addiction had gotten the better of him.

A few months after things opened up, I hit the gym again. I had been there about three weeks when I heard this familiar voice in a loud pitch, "God bless you! God bless you!"

I turned and saw Benedict. He was smiling, waving, and walking around the gym's second floor. He stopped at each exercise station, smiled, and God-blessed the fitness hopefuls. I think he had just got religion, as old-timers used to say. His joy beeped and bopped at a perky pace. He even blessed and waved at earbud-plugged people who couldn't hear him. Most people avoided eye contact with Benedict, and few others expressed mild annoyance with the interruption. It was clear the majority thought he was deranged, as he did look pretty messed up.

I overheard a guy say, "Only in San Francisco."

For the next four days, he repeated the same circuit, the same words, and the same crooked smile. On day five, his courage and joyful contagion reached a peak; as he walked down from the second floor, he leaned over the railing, and belted out to the one hundred or so exercisers on the first floor, "Hey everybody, God bless you! God bless you one and all!" Then he turned around and walked out. The next week as the Blessing of (saint) Benedict returned, I noticed a shift in the mood at the gym. People appreciated the consistency, felt endeared to him, and welcomed the much-needed kindness and friendliness.

Benedict didn't have much of anything. His clothes were second, maybe third-hand; his worn-out gym shoes probably came from a dumpster-dive. In the fifteen years I had known him, he had aged about thirty years. The hard life was etched in his wrinkles and cut to the bone. But his eyes were telling a different story. Amidst so much loss, they sparkled with new life, happiness, and joy. He was listening and messaging a different voice, God's happiness to 'one-and-all.' The contrast to the fit and youthful exercisers embarking on their maiden voyage of happiness was stark. Their eyes were vacant and urban lives jam-packed, but Benedict's joy, as absurd as it sounds, was the envy of the gym.

Full But Unfulfilled

Benedict offers us a free lesson on happiness. He led a happy, empty life with nothing but the clothes on his back and the belongings in his cart. This, contrasted with the stressed-out yet full-to-the-brim lives of the young gym rats, suggests that filling and fulfilling are very different things. We live as though we know what will make us happy, but our stress and vacant looks suggest otherwise.

Young and hopeful, we start our happy quest innocently enough. We look to the world around us. All signs and propaganda suggest happiness is wedded to wealth, travel, and accomplishments. We learn that a happy life is a "full" life. So, naturally, we overstuff life with, well, stuff. Anything advertisers, culture, and society slap a smile on, we take as the gospel of happiness; this is our first unhappy mistake.

Chasing one rapid dopamine hit after another—material wealth, adrenaline rushes, pleasurable sensations, gluttonous consumption, and soulless achievements—we don't have time to stop and check our happy meter. The world reinforces these assumptions by inundating us with endless happiness propaganda at every stoplight, media outlet, and social setting.

Here is where it gets ridiculous. When the happy fixes don't give us the same bump they once did, we mindlessly double down on our efforts, never pausing to ask if the pursuit of happiness has become a chase in hollowness. As a case in point, it's oddly entertaining that we know something like watching the news will depress us, make us angry, and leave us emotionally drained, but there we are each morning, faithfully filling up on negative slop and gulping down fear-peddling garbage.

We become so hardwired in our thinking that when someone with real experience voices that material wealth is a dead-end street, we shrug them off and say, well, maybe the Ferrari was a dead-end for you, but it will be the freeway for me.

We have been duped. We think more equals more. We put more activities in our schedule, more stuff in our house, and more experiences on our bucket lists. Even our day off is all on. Ever notice how we can return from an exhausting weeklong vacation more tired than when we left? Or how the house is cluttered with boring things that once made us happy? Or how our garage starts looking like one of those hoarder shows?

One insight from our review of Harvard's eighty-four-year study on happiness shocked us. *Every* decision we make in life, directly or indirectly, comes down to "Will this make me happy?"[15] And yet, all the pharmaceuticals, psychotherapies, and loneliness studies demonstrate evidence that our decisions are not making us happy!

We have collectively thrown everything and the kitchen sink at this problem of unhappiness. Every industry is in the happy business. Yet, despite countless books, thousands of university research projects, and the entire therapy sector, we are still living in the Age of Anxiety.

We long for something not just to fill but to fulfill us.

The greatest philosophers in Western history—Socrates, Aristotle, Cicero, Seneca—repeatedly philosophized that the good life (*eudemonia*), not material goods or physical pleasures (*hedonia*), leads to happiness. Though they disagreed on many subjects, on this, they stood pat.

Saint Augustine said that everything ends in boredom, and the great Christian philosopher Boethius added that finite things could not sustain the infinite joy we were made for. The truth is we are deathly afraid of emptiness; this is why Benedict's empty joy is so startling.

What does poor have to do with happy?

> *Happy are the poor in spirit for theirs is the kingdom of heaven.*
>
> —Jesus' first word on happiness.

Judas evidently missed the above lecture or wasn't paying attention to this point. Or perhaps he philosophized it with others but then neglected to put it in practice in his life. He fell prey to the deceptive thought that happiness could be bought, that the things that would really make him happy could be gained with thirty pieces of silver.[16] So after a three-year tutelage with Jesus he cashed in and betrayed his rabbi for money. What unhappiness in his life led him to first betray Jesus and then take his own life?[17] Perhaps his fixation with money stemmed from a place of distrust in God's abundance and goodness. Whatever the reason for his love of money it's evident that he never really understood Jesus' first word on happiness.

Often when we read 'poor in spirit,' we fixate on the word poor. Jesus, however, is not talking about materiality but about spirituality. The first followers of Jesus included both the wealthy and poor.[18] God's kingdom is not segregated along ethnic lines. Likewise, it's not segregated along economic lines. That said, Jesus doesn't say, happy are the rich in spirit. While we might never put the word poor and happy in the same sentence, he provocatively does. Hence, we are forced to think, wrestle, and argue with a joy described by the word poor.

Happiness is a Spiritual Matter

In his first oracle, Jesus clarifies that happiness is a spiritual matter. When Jesus says, "poor in spirit," he locates happiness in the spirit. Victor Frankl described the spirit from the concentration camps of Auschwitz as the pure self that emerged once the clothes were stripped from bodies, gold pulled from teeth, hair shaved from head, and possessions looted by the Nazis—"naked existence." All of us have this eternity existing under layer after layer of temporality. Thomas Merton called this the "le point vierge," the virginal center of nothingness, over which the blinking cursor of our personality flashes. God owns this inner backdrop, which is both reserved and compatible only with divine realities—love, peace, and joy.

Since divine happiness is spiritual, it cannot be contained in decaying things like cars or sustained by fleeting physical pleasures. Saint Augustine said, "A temporal thing is loved before we have it and grows worthless when we gain it, for it does not satisfy the soul, but the eternal is more ardently loved, the more it is acquired."[19] Joy is excessively infinite and needs an infinite house. Our spirit is the house built for joy. It's here that this divine laugh snugly fits. Joy thrives in the 'aha'—where God both happens to us, and we happen back to God.

Poor in spirit describes the *kind* of spiritual container befitting happiness. Jesus does not say, "Happy are the spiritual," "happy are the religious," "happy are the spiritually orthodox," or even, "happy are the Christians or Jews." He qualifies the kind of spirit with the word "poor." You can be spiritual, religious, Christian, or orthodox and arrogant, feeling as though you are needed and not needy, powerful and not powerless, entitled and not grateful. All of us have spirits, but not all of us are happy. There is an infinite amount of divine joy, but poor in spirit are those available to it. So how do we make our spirits poor?

There are two paths to poverty of soul: the voluntary and the involuntary.

Poor Means Needy (the involuntary path)

> *"God, have mercy on me, a sinner."*
> *—The Happy Sinner*
>
> *"God, I thank you that I am not like that man!"*
> *—The Smug Saint*
>
> *"God heard the sinner and ignored the saint."*
> —Jesus[20]

Jesus' world is divided into two groups: the upper class and the lower class. Within the lower class, there were four groups, but only two Greek words to describe them, *penés* and *ptōchoi*.[21]

The first word, *penés*, refers to peasants and those who lived paycheck-to-paycheck. The second word refers to the destitute

—the indigent and the disposables of society. This included criminals, beggars, mentally ill, and lepers. The *ptōchoi* were perceived as bottom feeders, who depended on handouts, unable to contribute to society.

Shockingly, Jesus does not say happy are the *penés* of spirit, but happy are the *ptōchoi* of spirit. Jesus uses *ptōchoi* to distinguish the poverty of spirit conducive to happiness. Due to their extreme losses or oppressive disadvantages, the *ptōchoi* were total dependents—they had no other recourse but God.

Ptochoi is the experience of loss; bankrupt-loss, bottom-of-the-barrel-loss. The loss can be a loss of privilege, freedom, health, relationships, or moral goodness. Losses frequently become bitterness, anger, and depression when they don't bring us close to God. But for those who face God with the loss, the result is a joyful awareness of God's abounding presence.

This seems counterintuitive. We tend to think the way to happiness is accumulation, but Jesus says loss makes room for infinite happiness. For example, losing a job may cause one to cry out to God and the miracle of God's presence in a moment of despair. As absurd as it may seem, even the loss of one's moral uprightness can turn into a desperate plea for God's mercy that shatters forth with a radiance of grace. In other words, experiences of loss are involuntary opportunities for embracing a poor spirit. Some internal gains are only acquired through external losses.

As we move toward the voluntary path of emptying, we remind you that happiness is more a practice than a goal.

Poor Means Empty (the voluntary path)

When Jesus was asked about The Way, to some, he replied, sell what you have (empty yourself) and follow me. When he invited the first four disciples to follow, they instinctively dropped nets (emptied their careers) and followed; the joyful prostitute emptied her alabaster box for Jesus' burial, and Jesus celebrated the little 'Widow's mite' given away as an act of emptying. Jesus speaks of emptiness squarely in the context of happiness, driving home the point that emptiness creates the conditions for heavenly happiness.

Jesus offers three secrets to making room for happy.

Halfway through the mountainside sermon, Jesus gave practical everyday handles to grip happiness.[22] He references Judaism's three commonly practiced spiritual disciplines—generosity, prayer, and fasting—as the way to voluntarily empty out the clutter of life. He picks up each discipline, turns it over and examines it, talks about the heart of it all, and then before setting the discipline down and moving on to the next, he says, "and the Father who sees in secret will reward you openly." We suggest that the open reward is forthcoming joy and happiness, eager to fill the space you created.

The spiritual disciplines make room for happiness in our physical, spiritual, and relational world. They are intentional ways of making a space for happiness.

Generosity

> *"When you give...your Father sees in secret and will reward you."*
>
> —Jesus.

The act of giving, another *makarism* of Jesus, is an act of happiness for the person receiving and for the person giving.[23] Why? When we give, we empty the stuff we have become inordinately attached to, and we free space to become reattached to God. At blinking speed, we cling to whatever we are holding onto. Living generously means we are clinging to God. The more we give and share, the more spacious our hearts and spirits become. As we let go of more and more stuff, we have room for more and more relationships. Generosity is an activity where we make room in the material space of our life for happiness. As we open our hands in giving, our hands are open to receive happiness—the Father's reward to the generous.[24]

Happy Practice:

- Buy someone's coffee in line behind you… and observe your happy meter.
- Tip someone more than expected…and then log your happiness.
- Practice consistent giving to your church or a non-profit.

Prayer

> *"When you pray...your Father sees in secret and will reward you."*
>
> —Jesus.

We know Jesus has a daily rhythm in mind because he says when you pray, say, "...give us *this day* our *daily* bread." A daily rhythm of prayer brings with it a daily happiness erupting from conversations with a Father who is keen to listen and holds on to our every word. Prayer requires that we carve out time, empty our schedule, and do nothing but wait on God. And Jesus says when we do this daily, in the closets of our life, we find our lives rewarded "on earth as it is in heaven." This counterintuitive act of stillness and silence—the realm of God's voice— develops the inner attentiveness necessary to be present for the serendipitous encounters with God's Spirit. God has placed a day of nothing, of no work, no frenzied activities into the creative order for this purpose precisely. We need emptiness in our day to recover our attentiveness and emptiness in our week to recalibrate our purpose. We need seasons of nothingness—holy days—to reflect on God's goodness. Prayer and meditation are places where we make room in our time for happiness.[25]

Happy Practice:

- Begin each morning with 10 minutes of stillness and silence in God's presence, then observe your happiness.
- Take one day off a week where you do nothing but play, rest, and relax. Trust God to work with you on the other six days. Observe your happiness.
- Pray the "Our Father" prayer daily, pausing at each stanza to riff on your feelings (Matthew 6:9-13).

Fasting

> *"When you fast...your Father sees in secret and will reward you."*
>
> —Jesus.

Jesus doesn't say "If you fast," but "when you fast" and thus assumes his students have a rhythm of abstinence. Fasting is not just a food thing, although it is that as well. We can fast from electronic gadgets, media, entertainment, alcohol, and pleasures. The word fasting reminds us that we tend to overconsume things, to look to food for comfort and escape. When we escape through consumption, we are out to lunch and unavailable for the joy of heaven. Fasting empties us in a very real and physical way. We feel lighter and more focused, internally and externally alert. The discipline engages us experientially in the truth that God is all we really need to be happy. What Jesus suggests here again is counterintuitive. Many people turn to food to make them happy when they are sad; Jesus says the real and inner reward is received from a generous Father while we surrender our appetites.[26]

Happy Practice:

- Fast for a week from the things preoccupying your time—social media, streaming online content, or the news.
- Practice an annual fast during the Lent season or a weekly fast day.

Saint Francis, "God's Fool," is considered the most joyful, jolly, and happy of saints. He is well known for preaching to birds, talking to cows, and laughing with his protégées. His radical vow of poverty, prayer, and fasting sustained this playfulness and joy. He understood his practice wasn't for everyone, but encouraged everyone to find what he called the Third Order, that is, their unique call to self-emptying.[27]

Notice in the refrains above "sees and rewards." The point Jesus makes is that God sees with an eye to reward. That alone puts a smile on our faces. Our Father is looking for ways to reward us, bless us, and delight in us.

Poor Means Available

Whew. That was a lot to unpack, but stick with us here, you happy little climber. We are almost finished. In the merriment and mirth miracle, John notes that Jesus chose six empty ritual cleansing basins to display his miracle of joy[28]. The empty cleansing basins are then repurposed as wine vats. This sequence from empty to repurposed happens when the empty situation faces Jesus.

If our emptiness faces ourselves, we may feel despair; when it faces others, we may feel envious. The miracle of joy finally happens when we bring our emptiness to face God. Under his caring eyes, our emptiness becomes filled with his generous vision and gracious presence. He repurposes unused and unwanted spaces for joy.

In the words of the Cana wedding coordinator, "The best

has been saved 'til *now*." This text gets frequently misquoted as, "he saved the best for last," implying we must wait *until the end* for the joy to erupt. That, however, is not what the host says. "You have saved the best 'til now" means the joy is immediate; it's now. We assume the wine ran out at the end of the party, but John says, "When the wine was gone." The wineless moment could have happened in the middle of the celebration.

This is part of what is so good about Jesus' happiness. We don't have to wait for some sweet-by-and-by moment, but the best is now. The moment we face Jesus with our emptiness, the best happens.

An Empty Start

We think the following prayer would be a fitting way to make some room for happiness.

You know the deepest parts of me.

I'm not even sure who I am sometimes.

You know the path I take.

I change my mind often and have walked so many different paths.

You authored the experiences for which I was made.

I am no authority, even on my own experiences and self-reports!

Before a word is formed on my tongue, you know it. I usually speak before I think.

You formed my inner being and knew the shape I was meant to take. I've spent a lifetime trying to get my soul in shape.

Search me, O God, show me what I am really longing for.

Awaken me to the reality I was created for.

And see if there be any shallow paths I am walking. Then, lead me in the merry way everlasting![29]

✿ Spaciousness

The happy emotion we are filled with when we empty ourselves out is spaciousness. Consider Benedict's blessing over the gym rats. His openness and spaciousness feel free. Imagine happily yelling into a gym full of focused exercisers, "God bless you one and all!" In the joy of spaciousness, you are unrestricted by your ego, unconfined by your stuff, and detached from everything but God. Spaciousness, like a lung-emptying exhale, is the sensation that follows a good purge, whether of a cluttered room or a releasing cry. Spaciousness is a kid, sprawled out on a creekbank, hands clasped behind his head, as he surveys his ever-expanding kingdom of crawdads, dragonflies, and frogs. Our inner and outer worlds are made for the joy of spaciousness; we joyfully discover that all the spaces we emptied out God has taken up.

❖ My Happy Declaration

Now I understand my emptiness is not to be resisted or feared. I have chosen to clear my table of clutter so that God can set it with a joyful spread! My emptiness will not need to be brought on by my willful desire for stuff. I choose to replace my gluttony for things to satisfy me, with empty rooms that God furnishes with the décor of joy.

➢ Up Next: Happy are those who mourn... (Matt 5:4)

We will pilgrimage through Happy Valley and sit with the topic of sadness. Does sadness have anything to do with happiness? Must we rid ourselves of sadness to be happy? And if so, how? The first test of authenticity for Jesus' happy way is how it manages sadness and sorrow. So, into the Valley, we go.

CHAPTER 5

THE VALLEY OF BACA

Freeing Our Sadness

The knowledge of the fallen world does not kill joy, which emanates in this world always, constantly, as a bright sorrow.

—Alexander Schmemann

Jeffrey: Crying while on an elliptical machine isn't very becoming, but there I was listening to Meister Eckhart's "Indestructible Joy," reflections from Germany's thirteenth century Christian theologian and boohooing away.[30]

James Finley, the author and clinical psychologist, told the story of a father whose daughter was diagnosed with terminal cancer. The little girl had a habit of taking his shoes while he was at work, traipsing around the house in them, then absentmindedly leaving his shoes scattered around the house. Upon returning from work, he often stumbled over the shoes and scolded her.

One day, he came home and found his dress shoes on the lawn, filled with rainwater. He sat her down and scolded her.

"Why do you keep doing this? Now look, you've ruined an expensive pair of shoes!"

She couldn't help herself and continued this annoyance. One morning, several months after the diagnosis, he found her on the floor of her room, dead. Heartbroken, he called the funeral home. When the funeral directors arrived, the dad headed down the stairs to let them in and saw one of her shoes lying on the landing, reminding him how she used to play with his shoes. The grief and anguish overwhelmed him in that moment. For weeks, he left her shoe untouched and unmoved from the stairs. Her shoe connected him to her and symbolized the preciousness of the simple things of life. He didn't know how to get through the grief, so he ignored and sidestepped it daily.

This was the story that brought my tears. It wasn't just the touching story, but it drew my attention to some area I was ignoring within me. As I felt the therapeutic grace of my tears, I knew that I too was sidestepping grief in my life. I knew the reason I was avoiding the shoes—I was ashamed to admit that I was sad and grieving.

A Sad Denial

The kind of sadness the bereaved father feels is anguish; the most excruciating kind of sadness. Neuroscientists and psychologists arrange human emotions into four categories—fear, anger, sadness, and happiness—and if we zoom in on each category, it opens a full spectrum of nuanced emotions. For example, sadness has well over sixteen different scales ranging from anguish to mildly disappointed.[31] Whether it's the sadness of abandonment or guilt or boredom, all of these emotions are alleged suspects in the case of our stolen happiness.

Like the father in our story, we sidestep pain, avoid our sorrow, and suppress our sadness. Our culture's presentation of constant smiles and filtered picture-perfect moments can leave us feeling like sadness is something to be ashamed of. In talking with students at universities, they lament the toxic positivity culture. Rather than be authentically present with their sadness, they pop artificial happy pills. They solve boredom with molly, weekday blahs with unprescribed Prozac, and dose the gnawing feeling of inferiority with something even stronger. The damage really stings during the "come down" when they feel like something is flawed in them for being so sad.

We don't need to read the scouting report on repressed sadness to know the physical and emotional toll this kind of avoidance takes on our well-being. Repressed sadness manifests in health issues, anxiety disorders, and even addiction cycles. Unaccepted and shamed, the bottled tears spoil, ferment, and eventually rot out our spirits.

Jesus' second word on happiness confronts the question of "what about all of us sad people? Can we have happiness too?" Jesus doesn't take the easy path of avoiding those who are sad but compassionately takes the space we just created in our heart and welcomes our sadness.

> *Happy are those who mourn for they shall be comforted.*
>
> —Jesus' second word on happiness

Jesus' inclusivity is remarkable. Happiness is for sad people too. Astonishingly, he begins his eightfold path to happiness, not with strengths and privileges, but with the unwanted conditions we all find ourselves in from time to time—states of sadness. His words give us permission to welcome the sadness.

Unscrambling, the Greek word for mourning, *pentheó*, clues us into solving the paradox behind this happy promise. Jesus uses the participle form of mourn (ongoing action), which can be translated as, happy are those *who are mourning.* This participle alerts us to the ongoing condition of mourning within the heart of all of us. We are born crying and we die crying and in-between is a continual brook of sadness. Jesus and the prophets connect this soul-grief to our exile from God. It's a subtle, yet profound, loss that we are in constant sorrow over.[32] Perhaps this is why we dam up the tears, or can't stop the tears, or can't find a reason for the tears. It's as if the abiding loss within us is far greater than any loss we've experienced.

A Sad Acknowledgement

Why do we humans try to replace sadness with happiness? We operate under the impossible assumption that we can only have ongoing happiness in the absence of sadness. We work hard to eradicate sadness from our lives. Yet, we fail repeatedly to make this once-and-for-all exchange. Beat down, we tiredly resign our lives to experiencing happiness in temporal bursts, in fleeting moments, and if we're lucky, in seasons or chapters of our life. Much to our little hearts' relief, Jesus acknowledges our sadness early on in his oracles. "Happy are those who *are mourning*." With that enigmatic statement Jesus is not only normalizing our human condition of sadness, but he is also hopefully declaring that happiness and sadness can co-exist. Perhaps he is even saying they *must* co-exist because in some way, at least here on earth, sadness has a way of authenticating joy.

Where does this insight come from? How does Jesus make this leap of connecting happiness with mourning?

Ashrei and Pilgrimage.

Wisdom Literature—Psalms, Proverbs, Job, Ecclesiastes, and Song of Songs—a section of books found in the Hebrew Bible, speaks frequently about the "Happy Life."[33] Of particular interest in the Happy Life musings was the Happy Prayer.[34] As a boy pilgrimaging to Jerusalem for Passover, Jesus would have sung these notes of happiness, mourning, and comfort.

Happy are those who dwell in your house;
  and praise you continually. selah
Happy the folk whose strength is in you,
  whose hearts are set on pilgrimage.
As they pass through the Valley of Baca,
  they make it a place of springs;
  the autumn rains also cover it with pools.
They go from strength to strength,
  till each appears before God in Zion.
O Lord of armies,
  Happy the man who trusts in you (Psalm 84:4-
7, 12)[35]

During the Babylonian wars, Jerusalem was exiled away from God's City and House. The Diaspora longed to return to God's house and happiness. And although most never made the trek, the Psalter kept hopes of pilgrimage alive. These pilgrim songs were sung in exile, while on pilgrimage, and upon ascending the steps to God's House.

Psalm 84, one such song, reflects on a pilgrim, one presumably scattered afar, who envies the "Happy Folk" and yearns for the happy life in God's house. Between the lines we sense the question, "Is there any happiness for those in exile?"[36]

The song sings hope when it choruses, "Happy the Folk whose hearts are set on pilgrimage." The notion here is that the turning of the heart toward home, the planning and prepping for the return fills the heart with happiness. Again, between the lines a few questions surface, "What if sadness and sorrow are part of the journey? How will we make it?"

Pilgrimage, for the few who could afford it, was long and costly. It was a once in a lifetime event, but it was not without its dangers. Bandits and thieves lurked along the road. Injuries, sickness, setbacks, and death were probable events. The songwriter addresses how all happy pilgrimages "pass through the valley of tears." Tears are unavoidable. But then, in poetic irony, the psalter exclaims that tears are our greatest resource. Tears bring strength, refreshment, resolve, and authenticity. The pilgrim comes to cherish the tears.

Exile is a living metaphor of our separation from God, and pilgrimage is the return journey. Pilgrimage gives us the language we need to locate our sadness. We aren't meandering along in meaninglessness, but on the map, we are right there in the Valley of Tears!

Beethoven faced numerous setbacks and challenges throughout his career, including the death of his mother, financial troubles, and the saddest of all, deafness. In a letter to a friend, he wrote, "I am always the unhappy man...Tears flow from my eyes and blood from my heart." The loss of hearing brought him to tears even publicly. The mournful affliction killed his career as a pianist. In the teary valley of deafness, Beethoven went from performer to composer. Completely deaf, he produced his most enduring symphonic composition, the Ninth Symphony. In the silence, he was freed to compose authentically, radically, and originally; he transformed classical music forever, leaving an eternal musical legacy in the wake of his sad affair with deafness.[37] Befittingly, "Ode to Joy," rings out during the Ninth Symphony's final movement in a lyrical crescendo of happiness:

> Joy! beautiful spark of divinity,
> Daughter from Elysium,
> We enter, fire-drunk,
> Heavenly, your sanctuary!
> Your magic binds again
> What convention strictly divides;
> All people become brothers,
> Where your gentle wing abides.[38]

Just as there is a stream of sadness in us, there can be a parallel flow of joy. In the Valley of Tears, we find both.

Kinds of Mourning.

Not all mourning is the same, but all mourning is welcomed and redeemed. Layered atop our unconscious sorrow are three kinds of conscious tears to which Jesus frequently ministered to—affliction (personal sorrow), repentance (spiritual sorrow), and compassion (communal sorrow).

Affliction. Affliction is the kind of mourning brought on by great personal suffering—a difficult divorce, the untimely death of a child, physical pain, abandonment and loneliness, the utter ruin of a happy life, or complete loss and bankruptcy. God hears and sees our tears of affliction. Unique to the Bible is the constant reminder that God is with the afflicted, oppressed, and crushed. From the first tears of a murdered soul crying from the ground to the groaning tears of Jesus in Gethsemane, we find one story of affliction after another: Job's total loss, Joseph's scathing betrayal, Hannah's desperate barrenness, Hagar's harsh excommunication, Tamar's rape. Yes, this happy oracle is for you.[39]

Repentance. What about those of us whose tears are self-inflicted? What of the tears of regret that come from the pain we have caused others and ourselves? Can these self-inflicted tears be redeemed? Consider David, the murderer and adulterer, or Jacob the deceiver, Paul the persecutor, or Mary the prostitute. Blessed are those who mourn tears of repentance for they shall be consoled.[40] Yes, this happy oracle is for you too.

Compassion. Compassion is the gift of "weeping with those who weep." Affliction and repentance mature into the sacred sadness of compassion. When we feel the pain of others and are moved to act, to love, and to express kindness, we are experiencing the emotion of God. The Hebrew Scriptures describe Yahweh's emotions most frequently as that of compassion. Jesus most pronounced and publicly displayed emotion was that of compassion.[41] He is moved with compassion to heal, to forgive, to teach, and to give. His compassionate tears flow at funerals, at hunger, at the shepherd-less flocks, and in prayer. And for our purposes here, it is interesting that compassion, while a sad emotion, is considered by many spiritual teachers to be the deepest form of happiness.

Jeffrey: As I headed home from the gym, I reflected on the shoes-on-stairs I had ignored. I had not grieved my divorce or accepted my own brokenness. I wanted to pick up the shoes, accept the losses, and be real with my new reality, but I was afraid to appear sad. Well-intentioned people were telling me to move on and be happy.

After a year of mourning, the father in our shoe story said a shift happened one day as he walked by a playground where little girls were playing with their dads. For the first time he was present with the sacredness of all children. Their laughs, giggles, and squealing delights filled him with an awareness of their preciousness. It was as if his deceased daughter had left a gift for him in her death, and his mourning had opened him to receive sacred preciousness. That wasn't all; he observed another gift she left him with. Whenever he heard of a parent losing a child, on the news or from a friend, he was filled with empathy, compassion, and mourning. She had given him the gift of empathy- something he never had before. Indeed, his mourning opened him up to her beautiful gift. Finally, he said, his mourning resulted in one final gift; the realization that her preciousness to him was immortal. Until the day he died, she would remain precious to him.

These final words made my sadness precious, acceptable, and the bearer of a richer and fuller joy. I said over and over, "lead me." The words gushed and gurgled; sobs gave way to extemporaneous words. "Lead me out of this mess, lead me into your path, lead me into your presence, I don't care where or how, I just want to be led by you." The joy emerged slowly, shyly, but steadily. At first, it was the joy of just being real and being okay with being real. Then, I realized God was present in that realness, in the truth of my hurt, and my broken faith. I was so absorbed in the moment, I didn't realize it, but I was experiencing an authentically happy state. I was mystified in how the sadness had morphed unexpectedly into a purified purpose. My tears felt like the gift of God to me and me back to God. In that estuary, the best part of me was being made available as a gift for others.

Sadness, the new normal

Can you recall a moment when your external presentation of self was operating in alignment with your internal reality? Maybe this is a moment when you were giving voice to your truth or being your genuine self. You walked away from the moment feeling real, authentic, even if a bit uncomfortable.

At the risk of sounding trite, happiness is most appreciated in contrast to, and even alongside, sadness. Sadness authenticates our happiness in a real way. When we accept our sadness whether in a moment, with a situation, or as an ongoing part of our human experience, we feel true to ourselves.

Archbishop Desmond Tutu tells the story of the assassination of one of his close friends in South Africa just before Easter. His emotions ranged from anger, despair, sadness, and fatigue. He says, "I broke down and [my wife] held me, like I was a baby." People called him and asked for spiritual counsel and answers. He walked into his little chapel, looked up toward heaven, and shouted out his anger at God, like Jeremiah. Later he says he learned that shouting out and naming the emotion, like "I HURT! I'M SAD!" releases these emotions from festering into wounds, and he attributes this to helping him guide his people into forgiveness and stopping cycles of violence.[42]

Confess the sadness. Perhaps it's shouting it out, naming the emotion, or simply journaling what kind of sadness you feel, why you feel it, and then telling yourself, "It's okay that I feel this way." Find your voice here, allow yourself the freedom of expressing what you feel as authentically as you can.

Pray the sadness to God. We face God with our sadness by simply including him and our sadness in the same sentence. Something as simple as, "God, I am sad!" connects our grief with the source of living joy- God. Once we have brought the sadness and the source of happiness together, we are readied for a miraculous comfort. Our real tears become the sacred ground of God's consolation.

Share the sadness with someone you trust. No one enjoys an Eeyore. By Eeyore, we mean a person, who is perpetually sad to the point of refusing to be consoled. Yet, Winnie the Pooh's happy band of forest friends never excluded their sad friend. We are conditioned to put on a happy face and leave sadness at the door. We are not suggesting that you cling to sadness like Eeyore, but that you share it with someone you trust. Until we learn to normalize the presence of sadness to ourselves privately and before others publicly, we will always feel bad about being sad. When we share our sadness, we make ourselves available for heavenly consolation.

Consolation

Most of our negatives amplifies more negatives. Fear becomes FEAR and sadness becomes SADNESS. Jesus comes along and offers his Presence to our sadness. As we accept both his Presence and our sadness, we encounter what Alexander Schmemann described as "bright sadness."

Consolation then, is the cross-pollination of sadness with happiness. When the shoes on the stairs unfold in compassion for a bereaved father, sadness and happiness come together. When courageous firefighters show up in the aftermath of a natural disaster, sadness and happiness come together. When following a mass shooting, a neighborhood lights candles, locks arms, and sings, "We shall overcome," happiness and sadness come together. When we look up from our tears and see a child's smile, when a life-sentenced prisoner receives an unexpected visit, when we feel that subtle nearness of God in our tears, we are happy, for there is no greater consolation.

❖ My Happy Declaration

I no longer believe that happiness is only achievable in the total absence of sadness. I will embrace my sadness as a guide who is leading me to a wide and open place of joy. I will thank my sadness for teaching me empathy and compassion. The sadness in my life will not engulf me, but will be comingled with the joy that God's comfort brings.

➢ Up Next: Happy are the meek…(Matt 5:5)

Is happiness something we take or receive? What do we do when happiness is taken from us, and how do we deal with the anger and anxiety? Can the world be a happy place with so many injustices? How does Jesus direct our demeanor? In the next chapter we will follow Jesus' happy trail into an inherited happiness.

CHAPTER 6

UNWILD MUSTANGS

Getting Our Character Right

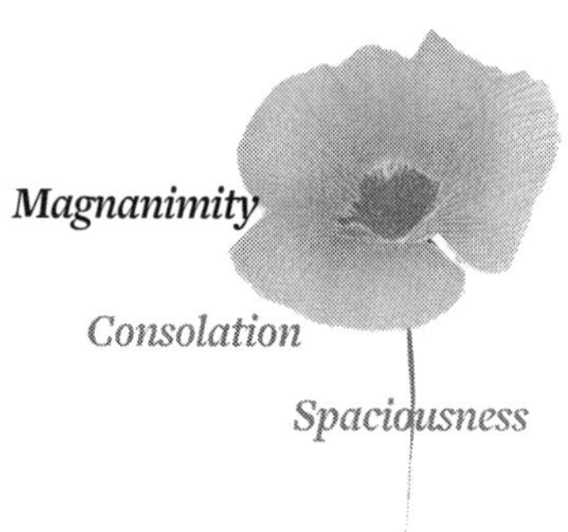

> *The meek man will attain a place of soul rest. As he walks on in meekness he will be happy to let God defend him. The old struggle to defend himself is over. He has found the peace which meekness brings.*
>
> —A. W. Tozer

Jeffrey: By all measurements, the pandemic wasn't really bad for us. We didn't lose anyone to death in our small church community, but our little neighborhood church dwindled from one hundred-sixty to twelve over the course of sixty-five weeks without an in-person gathering. Our beloved parishioners moved out of the City. I didn't blame San Francisco government's mandate, or our beautiful parishioners.

When the dust settled, we realized we could not continue to maintain the mortgage on our beautiful downtown church property. In eighteen months, we had gone through our savings and were forced to put the property on the market. The decision wasn't easy since land in San Francisco is hard to come by.

Our little flock took to praying, fasting, and surrendering this to God. We put a "for sale" sign up on the building and went in and out of escrow four times over the course of the next nine months. Letters from the bank and phone calls from mortgage officers hounded us. We were about to lose a property we had owned for two decades.

One day after telling Pastor Edwin, an Indonesian pastor-brother, who shared our space, that we had to sell, he got all choked up and kept saying, "So many, many, memories here."

After our conversation, as I ascended the stairwell, I looked up and there was a rainbow of colors dancing across the walls. The mystical art show was produced by the sun and a metallic object dancing in the wind. I sat down on the stairs and melted, it felt like there was a witness to my struggle. I know it's silly, but when you're going through it, you'll take any sign of hope. I didn't know what it meant, but it was assuring, a small promise of hope in the midst of so much loss.

When the call came that an investor wanted to buy the property, cash, and with only a thirty-day contingency, I knew this was it. As my realtor delivered the contract, he informed me that the buyer was the owner of a sex club. Yes, you read that right. SEX CLUB! I felt punched in the gut.

How was it that industries with a reputation for trafficking and exploitation had so much money and we, a people called to love and be a symbol of heaven in San Francisco, had nothing?! I envied the buyer's capital investment power and lamented our enslavement to the bank. Psalm 37 prophetically challenged me, "Fret not yourself because of evil doers neither be envious . . ."

Many well-intended friends advised me to take the money and go. Six million in cash would resolve all our financial problems in an instant. Others said I should go public and decry the bank. Bring the media into the picture and cancel the bank for taking advantage of us in the pandemic. We were being tested. I knew it. Did we trust the sex club was our answer? Or did we trust the social media influencers were our answer? Or could we let go and trust God?

Psalm 37 directed us. We knew the answer was not money, influence, media, or public pity. The answer was radical trust in God. With or without the building, we, the people, were the true temple of God and that could never be taken away. Whatever happened to the property was not for us to fret over. We responded in two ways. First, we pulled the property off the market. We would rather the bank have it than a sex club. Second, we refused social media shaming of the bank. We wanted to be the people of God who loved and not people of the property who got ugly. 1337 Sutter Street was in God's power, to release or to save. Our demeanor and heart were our responsibility to steward. I cannot describe here the joy that washed over me in that moment of relinquishment.

We are a nation of pursuers and we stand as a beautiful beacon of pursuit to the world—"life, liberty, and the pursuit of happiness." Pursuit is not a bad thing; in fact, it can be lovely. Think of God's pursuing love of His children.

However, when pursuit morphs into aggression, our once healthy drive takes on a life of its own, grabbing, getting, hacking, and ransacking everything in its path. Suddenly, we find ourselves caught in the ugly middle of this hostile world in which we are either seizers or seized from.

For early American immigrants, land became the happiness that they pursued. The Western Expansion with its promise of free land and settlers' rights, was just one sad story of happiness run amok with Native Americans suffering untold injustices along the Trail of Tears. Settlers pursued happiness at the expense of taking land from the tribes who had inhabited it for centuries.

If happiness, as we are told, must be seized, we quickly legitimize whatever it takes to secure it as our inalienable right. After all, this is the way the happy game is played and won.

This pervasive whatever-it-takes grab at happiness can be seen in schoolyard bullying, high school cyber-bullying all the way through to corporate intimidation and political bullying. Before long, happiness is no longer a pursuit, but a pillaging and plundering of our neighbor and environment.

This is not a new problem created by the American Dream, but as old as humanity's pursuit of happiness.

Cain *takes* Abel's life. It eliminates the competition.

Jacob *seizes* his brother's birthright. It's the fastest way to wealth.

David *takes* Uriah's wife. It's an immediate path to pleasure.

Ahab *defrauds* Naboth. It's the easiest path to his own winery.

In a world where happiness depends on tilted scales and unfair advantages, we may wonder if there is a way to happiness that doesn't involve cutthroat ambition and step-on-their-toes assertiveness. Is the big slice of happy pie only for the conniving, opportunistic strong-armers, while the weak get the unhappy leftovers?

Was this what Jesus had in mind when he talked about inheriting the earth?

> *Happy are the meek for they shall inherit the earth.*
>
> —Jesus' third word on happiness.

Jesus' hillside audience was living in a land occupied by a foreign world power, taxed by an enemy, and oppressively controlled. The prevailing social sentiment hailed *when we get our land back and have our freedom,* we will be happy and blessed. Debates about how to reclaim the land divided the population up into factions—terrorist fighters, wilderness expats, futility conformists, wealthy collaborators, and then the poor who were simply confused and caught between all these groups.

The relevancy of Jesus' happy claim jars his students back to the Psalms. In Psalm 37 human-traffickers, wealthy slumlords, and oppressive land-magnets take more than their fair share. The Psalter understood the ugliness of an unfair world where happiness is taken at another's expense. David and Asaph bear historical witness to the anger and frustration we feel when we have been vandalized and victimized.[43] In several beautiful prayers we are given words of lament as we grieve our plight.

> Do not *fret* (when the unjust succeed)
> Do not *envy* (when the opportunists get ahead)
> Do not have *anxiety* (when the selfish succeed)
> Do not be *angry* (and do something to get even)
> Do not be *frustrated* (and resign in self-pity)
> Do not get *vengeful* (and repay evil with evil)

Then in verse 11, the "meek shall inherit the earth." And just in case we miss this point, the poet reinforces this truth five times—not the aggressive, angry, envious, or vindictive, but the meek "dwell in the land forever."

Jesus in his third happy oracle quotes verbatim from this wisdom text.[44] He changes nothing, but rather reinforces that happiness is not about seizing back ownership, fighting for national freedom, or political activism. Happiness is about meekness.

Meekness becomes Jesus' word of happiness for those us who feel defrauded, outpaced, or disadvantaged in our chance for happiness. Meekness is the righted happy pursuit. Meekness is the way we pursue. In the Psalmist's answer, happiness is about how we pursue and not what we pursue.

So, what is meek? Meek (*praus*) appears four times in the New Testament. Three times are in Matthew, and all have to do with Jesus. Eugene Peterson, the poetic translator behind the Message Translation says, translators have a "huge problem of vocabulary." We think of meekness as gentle or humble, but this alone does not account for the "coiled energy of those who possess meekness."[45]

Hermeneutics, the science of interpretation, suggests we use the *first mention principle,* when defining infrequently used words or concepts found in sacred texts. The first mention of the word meek in the Hebrew Bible simply states, "Now the man Moses was very meek, above all the men which were upon the face of the earth." With this mention we have a clue; a man who embodies meekness.

A Case Study in Meekness

Few Bible stories start with one's birth and follow them to their death. When we find such a story it includes significant character development with contact points, hidden templates, relatable conditions, and a bastion of wisdom for our own human journeys. Moses is one such story and his cultivation of meekness is one such template. The relevant backstory includes the following character developments:

Moses kills an Egyptian in anger and rage.
Moses flees as a fugitive to the Midian wilderness.
Moses is called by God years later.
Moses says no.

> *"Who am I?"* (insecurity)
> *"Who will believe me?"* (incompetency)
> *"I have a speech impediment."* (disability)
> *"Send someone else." (inadequacy)*

Moses smashes the Sacred Stones out of anger at Israel. Moses beats a rock because he's so angry at Israel.

The point is Moses is stubborn, angry, and insecure. Yet, he somehow works through all these issues to merit being called the meekest man on earth.

Meekness is Strength Under Control

The story where the narrator tells us that Moses is the meekest man has to do with a defamation case brought against Moses by his sister and brother. They accuse Moses of disqualifying himself as their leader for marrying an African. They usurp his seat of leadership and oust him. Miriam and Aaron rationalize, "Has the Lord indeed spoken only through Moses? Has he not spoken through us also?"

Moses doesn't get angry, defensive, or take matters into his own hands. There is not even an attempt to explain or disprove their claims. Smack dab in the middle of Moses' resolute silence and surrender, the Scripture says, *"Now the man Moses was very meek."*

The anger issues of previous years have been tamed. He doesn't cling to his authority. He's magnanimous and broad-shouldered in his godly trust. He's no longer inhibited by his speech impediment nor self-conscious of his leadership abilities.

We see a combination of qualities at play in his meekness. He demonstrates the intangibles of being able to encounter attacks without getting defensive. Miriam and Aaron are cruel and mean, and yet he doesn't become harsh or rash. Moses doesn't have to be in control and doesn't seek glory. He willingly empowers others even when it costs him his own power. He disdains revenge. He has nothing to prove. If you have ever attempted to act out any of these qualities then you KNOW that meekness is not weakness, but strength under control.

When we compare young Moses to the elder Moses,

it's apparent which one is happier, more peaceful, and more magnanimous.

Happy Failure

Moses stumbles and fails his way into meekness. We need to be clear on this. Meekness is not the outcome of our spiritual accomplishments and successes, but an alchemy of all our failures. Meekness is a lesson our failures teach us, or perhaps better said, a lesson we are finally willing to learn.

We fail our way into the happy land. *Felix Culpa*, the theological term for this, means "happy failure." Our failures, when surrendered to God, become the silly source of much of our happiness. Julian of Norwich expressed happy failure like this, "First the fall, then the recovery from the fall, both are the mercy of God." Somewhere in this tripping and bumbling God takes our hand and turns the stumble into dance.

Failure is the only experience that prepares our heart for meekness. As we persevere through the mistakes and wrongs, we see how our faulty attitudes are not aligned with the truest and purest parts of our heart.

Abe Lincoln is often referred to as the meekest president of the United States. His path was fraught with failure, disappointment, and ridicule. He was fired from his first job, failed at business, and his political life was more of the same—defeated six times before he was finally elected President. But in the United States' most vulnerable and needy moment, it was his meekness, not his intelligence or his aggression, that the country needed. Historians point out his meekness was the strength that reunited the North and South, and it was his humble perseverance through failure that forged the might meekness in him.

The Making of Meekness

Martin Buber, the great Jewish philosopher, and Nobel Peace Prize nominee, wrote about meekness in his popular work, *Ten Rungs*. Using Jacob's ladder as a metaphor for the rungs that ascend the heights of God's joy, Buber placed meekness on that final rung just before the final redemption. Buber reflecting on Moses' meekness asks, "How could [he be meek]?" He claims it was the *Presence* of God that made Moses meek. Between Moses' murderous rage and his siblings' attempted coup, is scene after scene of Moses encountering the presence of God.

There's the Burning Bush, Fiery Mount Sinai, and the Glory of God in the cleft of the rock. God rubs off on Moses. The one consistent context we see repeatedly is he's tasked with an assignment only God can accomplish. So, he has to be both bold and humble: meek.

Moses comes to realize God is the leader, deliverer, and miracle worker; he's just a tagalong. He stutters before Pharoah, and God still delivers. He stalls before the Red Sea, and God still parts it. He's flummoxed by the unclean water and food supply issues. His limitations keep him in constant conversation with God. This continual interplay of personal liabilities, prayer, and Presence forge a happy dependence into his soul.

Perhaps now we see why humility alone is an incomplete description of the word meekness. Anytime we say yes to God-sized challenges, there is a humble strength, a courageous modesty, a magnanimous meekness. Now there are two words you rarely see in the same sentence: strong and meek. Like Moses, we can develop the might of meekness and receive its happy repose.

The Power of Meekness

The third happy oracle turns on this word, "inherit." Jesus doesn't say, "The meek will merit the earth," as though we earn it. Neither does Jesus say, "The meek will take the earth," as though we muscle our way into ownership. Merit leads to entitlement and ingratitude. Taking leads to hard-heartedness. Both attitudes are anything but happy. What Jesus says is the meek will inherit the earth. Everything from land, to blessings, to callings are inherited by God. The way of being gifted is God's happy way.

Meek people are powerful people because they aren't entitled, anxious, or conniving. They realize the earth is something to be inherited, not something to be exploited, demanded, owed or taken. The meek are children of their Father, and he is passing on an inheritance to them.

We are not much different from those early hillside followers. Land still symbolizes security, identity, wealth, and posterity. Wars are still waged over land, and genocide executed in the seizure of lands. Refugees in camps and boats, walking over mountains and sleeping beside roads, tell the story of the extreme measures the unjust will go to for a piece of land. Yet Jesus maintains that in the end the meek are quietly inheriting it all, and this inheritance is not exclusive. He offers meek refugees and humble homeowners alike an inheritance, too.

Jeffrey: Within four weeks of our decision to take the property off the market, Wesleyan Investment Foundation stepped up and offered us a loan. Nine-months of interest only payments. They made an exception for our flagging finances and pandemic depleted resources because they felt strongly about not losing a kingdom footprint in San Francisco. Yes, in a very literal sense meekness won the day and inherited the earth.

The focus of this oracle is on meekness and the happiness it produces in our lives. Many commentators and thought leaders have opinions on what it means to "inherit the earth," but for our purposes, let's rest in the fact that meekness draws to itself an inheritance. Jesus doesn't say, "The meek will one day be happy once they inherit the earth," but "Happy are the meek." Meekness is present tense happiness. What or when the inheritance happens is beyond the scope of this chapter. For now, we know meekness is mighty for it is the happy attitude that calls forth the inheritance of God.

Happy Tribe

Jesus likened his new happy city to a woman mixing flour, leaven, oil, and salt into a ball of dough. Underscoring the role of the leaven, Jesus said, it was "hid in three measures of flour, till it was all leavened" (Matthew 13:33). We love that Jesus uses the image of a mother baking bread, there is something disarming and meek with this picture. The meek are the leaven, hidden away, in the world, transforming both themselves and the world into living bread. Their smallness, stuttering through speech impediments, and quaking before fiery mountains, is strong and bold in God.

The world brushes over the link of happiness with meekness in search of something more attractive or profound. Jesus, however, plants happiness in the unnoticed and unpopular soil of the ordinary. Meekness is that extraordinary happiness hidden in plain sight of the ordinary.

❁ Magnanimity

What happy emotion is given to those who finally come into possession of meekness? Magnanimity. We chose this word as the emotional descriptor for meekness partially because of its poetic use by Emily Bronte, Ralph Waldo Emerson, and John Keats. The word is boldly vast, yet humbly vacant like the sky. William Wordsworth in his poem "The Character of the Happy Warrior" celebrates the magnanimous happy soul.

We sense magnanimity when we stand in an open field with an un-wild mustang. We feel awed by her bruising strength, yet safe in her bridled will. We respect the flash of force that could crush us in seconds, yet we're drawn to her angelic eyes, assuring us all her strength is harnessed. The once volatile animal now puts off a sense of magnanimity. We brush her muscular neck and sense she can connect with us; she can offer affection and, in some way, even heal us. Lingering, we come to feel safe in her strength. A tamed mustang is magnanimous.

In our day-to-day life, magnanimity is the feeling we have when we cheerfully give or when our coworker gets the promotion we wanted, and we genuinely congratulate him. It's the emotion that holds our anger in check when someone cuts the grocery line or takes our parking spot. It's the feeling we get when we take the high road and respond with kindness.

The magnanimous are confident of their inheritance. Their happiness is no longer taken hostage by fits of rage, bouts of anxiety, and clouds of self-doubt, all of which bully out the happy child. Instead, they are noble, temperate, and restful in God's happy flow.

❖ My Happy Declaration

Because I have learned that meek doesn't mean weak, but strength under control, I will surrender my character to the forging of meekness within me. Though I may have physical, emotional, financial, or influential strength to dominate, control, intimidate or crush others, I will not. I choose to love, prefer, and favor others. My reward to inherit the earth means I do not need to strive or to merit it. Happiness will overflow!

➢ Up Next: Happy are those who hunger and thirst for righteousness...(Matt 5:6)

Where does the pursuit of happiness actually lead? Why are we less happy when we indulge in a craving? How can our hunger drive us into the voice of God? What are we really hungry for?

CHAPTER 7

HEALTHY HAPITITES

Getting Our Appetites Right

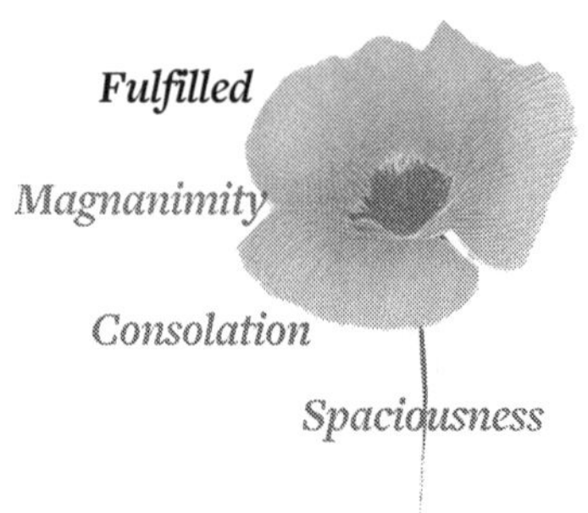

Happy are they who have the promise that they shall be filled, for the righteousness they receive will be no empty promise, but real satisfaction.
—Dietrich Bonhoeffer

Jeffrey: My son, Jed, was struggling with grades his sophomore year of high school. Understanding the rigors of academics, I sat down with him for a pep-talk about doing better in school, building my case around how university admissions were highly competitive. He stared at the ground while I talked. I paused and let the silence fill the room, waiting for his response. When he finally looked up from the floor, his face was strained and stressed. With a quivering voice he said, "I'm doing my best. You don't understand what it's like being a kid in my world. The pressure is too much. Teachers. Coaches. Family. Friends. I feel so much pressure to get into a good college. And social media makes you feel like you're not good enough or important enough."

His tears joined in, "I try so hard, but other kids are much smarter than me. I study on the bus after our Lacrosse games, and the guys always ask me why I'm spending time studying when cheat-sheets and other cheating hacks are available. Dad, I am not a cheater, I won't cheat, I just wish I was smarter. What college will want me? I'm just average."

I walked away from that conversation proud of Jed but angry with the world. Jed walked away from that conversation and turned to God. Off and on, and unbeknownst to me, he cried out to God for help for a full year. His desperation grew with each test and class.

About a year later, Jed, wrapping up his junior year, posted the following on GoFundMe.

gofundme

It's 2am. I'm in my dad's office studying for another test. The school workload, plus everything else . . . I'm so overwhelmed. I'm constantly stressed with, *what college will accept you? Your ACT and SAT scores place you in the middle-bottom of the pack. What's wrong with you*? I'm failing, I don't want to be a failure.

I just hate that I'm not smarter. What's wrong with me?!?!?! I'm so angry and sad, not even God is with me. *I'm all alone. If I could just hear a voice, get some message from God, I need some kind of miracle!*

Tonight I cried out of frustration and pain, then I looked over at my dad's bookshelf. Something happened, one book stood out to me. I grabbed it. It opened easily to this page:

"Do not keep striving for what you are to wear or what you are to eat, and do not keep worrying about college and your career, for the world strives and strives for these things. Your Father knows that you need them. Instead, strive for the kingdom of God, and these things, all of them, will be given to you as well."

I'm not sure, but I think God spoke in that moment.

My stress is gone. I'm confident of what I'm going to do. I was told to seek God's kingdom first and he would direct my college, my life, and my future. I will do this, and not worry about the rest.

My best friend wanted me to go with him to Turkey this summer, but I have decided to "strive for the Kingdom," and not strive for a good time with friends. I'm going to go to Bangkok and work with refugee kids, that sounds like God's Kingdom to me. This trip to Thailand is my attempt at seeking God's kingdom first with my life. **Will you help fund me?** 46

The story of what happened, a surprise of joy that I'll pick up later, highlights the happy adventure that can happen when we courageously redirect our hunger and thirst into God.

No doubt about it, food makes us happy! Consider the behemoth food industry! From cookbooks, to cooking and baking shows, culinary degrees, to foodie fusions, foodie towns, and foodie people. There is nothing like watching a kid who really appreciates food.

Recently in Dallas, at Kenny's Wood Fired Grill, while waiting for our meal, a nearby family—mom, dad, and three daughters—dove into their appetizers with gusto. Their buttery popovers came out first with their steaming hot gooiness. The doughy smell, gooey texture, and chef hat shapes of the popovers transfixed the youngest girl. She artistically broke open the popover, brushed butter throughout the crusty cave, and patiently waited for the melting effect to complete. Then with eyes closed, and head slightly tilted, she savored the experience. She smiled a *this-is-the-life* smile and put on a show that was every bit as valuable as our meal. When she came to, she insisted her dad close his eyes and open his mouth. She giggled as he along with her enjoyed the miracle of food. The entrees and desserts brought similar reactions from the entire family. Happiness was all over their satisfied faces.

If empty bellies were the only kind of hunger humans knew, the answer to our cravings would be obvious. Food. However, we humans have ravenous appetites for so much more than food and the satiation to our hungry growls seems more complex than a piece of bread and glass of water.

Mis-directed Hunger, Insatiable Growls

The wide scale of our hunger can be witnessed in everything from our palate to our pocket, our work-life to our sex-life, intellectual aha moments to physical achievements. Growling, our hungry drive grabs the steering wheel of our life turning this way and that in search of happy satiation. The erratic and temporal nature of our drives can be seen as we speed from one happy stop to the next. From our choice of food to our choice of car, from our career path to our spouse, we repeatedly choose what we *think* will make us most happy. Yet depression, loneliness, and boredom wreak havoc in our world. This inability to seize the happy life is shocking since just about any decision we humans make we make with happiness in mind.

After all our happy fails, whether the failed-marriage, the unfulfilling job, or the debt-inducing purchases, we should admit that our drives are not to be trusted with the steering wheel of life. Additionally, we don't consider the *temporal* nature of any good and wonderful thing. Saint Augustine said, "everything no matter how wonderful ends in boredom." The sad reality is our *pursuit* of happiness overpromises and underperforms. As the longest study on happiness revealed, "We humans are often bad at knowing what is good for us."[47]

Listen to the prophets sitting in recovery circles in an AA meeting. They know all too well the vanishing act of happiness. Our cravings return less happiness each time we consume them.

The truth is we do not get a choice in whether we hunger and thirst, only what we hunger and thirst for, but as Howard Moskowitz, Harvard psychophysicist said, "we cannot always explain what we want deep down."[48]

What we want deep down cannot be explained in terms of pleasures, achievement, popularity, or aesthetics. With his fourth word on happiness, Jesus aligns our appetite with what we want deep down.

> *Happy are those who hunger and thirst after righteousness, for they shall have their fill.*
>
> —Jesus' fourth word on happiness.

Many of Jesus' impoverished listeners needed no imagination for this fourth word on happiness, as they were well acquainted with hunger and thirst. The stories of famine and drought were a thick part of developing the character of heroes like Joseph and Elijah. But to hear that hunger and thirst can be a happy condition, well, that was unheard of. Whoever started a sentence with, "happy are those who hunger and thirst..."? What leads Jesus to make such an audacious claim about an unhappy condition? When we are hungry, we are hangry, not happy!

Hunger and Thirst

Where does Jesus get the idea of connecting hunger and thirst to happiness? Jesus in a prior scene prays and fasts for forty days and nights. As he nears the end of his fast, Satan tempts him to turn stones into bread. Mustering every ounce of inner strength, Jesus shockingly uses his hunger for food to drive him to the voice of God.

> Man shall not live by bread alone,
> but by every word that comes from the mouth of
> God. (Matthew 4:4).

Hunger and thirst are basic, God-given human drives; they trigger our survival instincts. But, according to Jesus, that is not all they do. Jesus says they also signal our spiritual needs. Jesus demonstrates this during his temptation. The point he makes is that we live by them—but not by them *alone*. Bread fills the growling stomach, but doesn't fill the growling soul.

Jesus' experience with hunger and thirst is a teaching moment for all of us. He repurposes his forty-day hunger to drive him to the voice of God. He knows the human fallacy is to always obey our hunger and thirst. He disrupts this dictatorship and guides our drives to God. In effect, he is saying: our path to personal happiness is to live by God's voice and not by bread alone.

Jesus draws a line connecting our 'hunger and thirst' to our happiness. Notice he does not say, "Happy are those who no longer hunger!" or even, "Happy are those whose stomachs are full!" Instead, Jesus provokes us to consider how the happy ones are those who have reconnected their hunger and thirst to God. With the hungry metaphor, Jesus introduces us to what our creatureliness really craves.

"Hunger and thirst for righteousness" echoes Isaiah 58's famous oracle on righteousness, fasting, and joy.

Isaiah is dealing with a people who are unhappy, spiritually numb, and unaligned with God. Yet they do spiritual things like fasting, praying, and observing all the temple rituals. On the one hand, they are hyper-religious, but on the other they exploit their workers, gossip, oppress the poor, and justify violence.

God challenges them to hunger and thirst for neighborly justice.

> Is not this the fast that I choose:
> to loose the bonds of wickedness,
> to undo the straps of the yoke,
> to let the oppressed go free,
> and to break every yoke?
> Is it not to share your bread with the hungry
> and bring the homeless poor into your house;
> when you see the naked, to cover him,
> and not to hide yourself from your own flesh?
> (Isaiah 58:6-7)

Isaiah then promises their happiness will return when they seek righteousness.

> then shall your light rise in the darkness
> and your gloom be as the noonday.
> And the Lord will guide you continually

and satisfy your desire in scorched places
(Isaiah 58:10-11).

Getting It Right

Dikaiosune, the Greek word, translated as "righteousness" needs some rounding out. If we think of the term within an ecological context, it means all the parts are aligned and in a harmonious relationship. The universe is righteous in the sense that the earth balances at the perfect distance from the sun, rotates at the perfect speed, and revolves in perfect syncopation with the universe. Righteousness means alignment and alignment means flourishing.

By bringing happiness and righteousness together, Jesus is saying that happiness needs to be properly aligned to flourish.

In Judeo-Christian thought, righteousness has a vertical and horizontal axis. We are vertically aligned when we are right with God, and we are horizontally aligned when we are right with each other. This is why *dikaiosune* is translated sometimes as justice and at other times as righteousness.

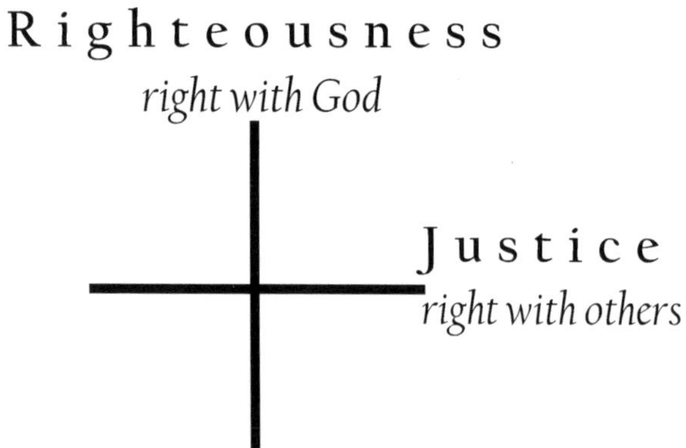

One final word here is in order; Jesus taught that being out of alignment with one leads to unalignment with the other. In one word, *dikaiosune,* he sums up both alignment with heaven and with earth, with God and with each other.

Righteousness is seeing God rightly

> *Noah was a righteous man, blameless in his generation*
>
> —(Genesis 6:9).

Noah is the first human called righteous. Curiously, we know nothing of his spiritual practices or his doctrinal beliefs. He's blameless, but there's no Ten Commandments, let alone a Bible, to follow. So, what's to account for his rightness with God if we don't know his spiritual practices, doctrinal beliefs, or the rules he's obeying? And how is it that his generation is evil and blameful if, similarly, they don't have the Ten Commandments?

Genesis simply says that Noah "found grace in the eyes of the Lord" (6:8 KJV). Noah looked into the eyes of God and saw grace. When Noah prayed, he sensed favor, tenderness, mercy, and compassion. Noah is righteous because his view of God is not skewed, distorted, or perverted. He lives, as we all do, in the light of who he sees God to be. And because his eyes see God's grace, he experiences grace. How we see God is how we see all of life, and this especially includes our perspective on happiness. If we see God as a killjoy, we will live as either killjoys or as godless hedonists. If we see God as absent from our personal yearning for happiness, we will feel powerless or helpless in our happiness. Our worldview of God and our relationship with happiness are inextricably linked. The happiest people see God as happy.

God is gracious, so Noah hears a gracious warning. God is merciful, so Noah builds an ark of mercy. Grace is spacious and inclusive, so Noah builds a spacious and inclusive animal shelter. See the connection between rightness with God meaning rightness with the world?

On the other hand, the Floodsters don't get God. Their bloodlust and beastliness are the incarnation of their gods. They are not right with God and hence not right with the world.

What we see in God, we reflect to the world.

Righteousness is trusting God rightly

> *And he believed the Lord, and he counted it to him as righteousness.*
>
> —(Genesis 15:6)

Abraham is the second man called righteous. Again, we have no account of spiritual practices, or creedal commitments. What we do have is God appearing to Abraham and informing him that he wants to do something good for Abraham.

> *"I will bless you and make your name great,*
> *so that you will be a blessing.*
> *I will bless those who bless you . . .*
> *and in you all the families of the earth shall be blessed."* (Genesis 12:2-4)

Abraham simply trusts God's goodness—that's it. Abraham believes in this goodness and God chalked it up as righteousness! As his story unfolds, we see this righteousness leads him naturally, as it should, into a just life with his neighbors and all the families of the world.

Can you see the happy connection? God wants to do good things for us! God wants to bless, make us a blessing, and bless the world through us. The happiness and joy flows to us, in us, and through us to the world.

Path of Righteousness

The path to righteousness can be an unwieldy one. In our desire to connect our growling hearts to righteousness, we can step in some muddy puddles along the way. We humans tend to complicate things. Perhaps, the omission of creeds and commandments in the Noah and Abraham stories are a clue to the simple kind of righteousness we are after.

Religio-Righteousness. "My religion makes me right with God."

This is characterized by dividing the world into people who believe about God like us and people who don't. When we are dogmatic about our beliefs and righteous standards, we are attempting to find happiness through religio-righteousness. We feel arrogant, spiritually superior, theologically aloof, and justified in our moral segregation. This may offer some kind of corrupt happiness, but not the pure happiness God has in mind for us. Righteousness without justice eventually takes the shape and form of religious elitism. Being out of touch with justice for others tends to lead towards prejudice and a demand that everyone pull themselves up by their bootstraps like we did.

Unrighteousness. "I don't need righteousness."

When we are spiritually lethargic, socially unaware, and self-absorbed, we are unrighteous. Our attempt to find happiness through self-absorption is unrighteousness. A human relationality that has no justice and no righteousness is non-dimensional. When we are without heart for the world and without heart for God, we are essentially heartless. This eventually leads to anything from boredom to hedonism, from addiction to loneliness. Most certainly, it dead ends in un-happiness.

Self-righteousness. "My goodness makes me right with the world."

The attempt to find happiness by comparing what is right with us to what is wrong with others is called self-righteousness.

This is a significant cause of unhappiness. Doing justice without a sense of God's joy, grace, and love will have us side-stepping into a self-righteousness that says our good deeds and compassionate politics elevates us above those who don't do justice. We open the door for superiority and pride which often fill our hearts with bitterness and anger toward those who lack compassion or a sense of justice. Finally, when our efforts fail to produce lasting change or when we labor away unnoticed and unappreciated, we battle with compassion fatigue or worse yet feelings of ineptitude.

Faith-Righteousness. "I trust in God to gift me with His righteousness, and I live this out responsibly with the world."

The genius of this perspective is it keeps us happy. On the one hand, we remain humble because it's not our righteousness but God's. On the other hand, we are grateful for this gift. The humble gratitude inoculates us against arrogance and entitlement. With God's righteousness we act right toward the world. We are happy because we are no longer religiously striving and socially stressed out.

If you see your righteousness as an *"un," "religio,"* or *"self,"* and want to reconnect with the faith-righteousness, a simple way to get going with this happy attitude is to imagine Jesus blessing us with his righteousness. Let's try something here; you can do this with any happy attitude, but we want you to experience the realness of it with this one.

Pray "God I want to be right with you. I want to be rightly aligned with my world. I want to want this like water and food." (sit in the reflection of this prayer for a moment).

Imagine Jesus blessing you. He looks into your eyes, and he says these words, "I bless you with righteousness." Hear this over and over, until it drowns out your doubts, your feelings of unworthiness, and your questions about your past or your abilities.

Say, "Thank you. I accept that happy blessing. Just as you were so I am in the world."

Take Notice. Our experience is that as we are aligning with God, we feel tugged to acts of kindness, works of justice, or a labor of love. This is the alignment of happiness. Respond to this today. If you don't sense anything, keep engaging in this little exercise— it will happen.

Fast. For those who felt inspired by the Isaiah 58 section, we would encourage you to investigate the joy that awaits you in fasting. The fast doesn't have to be food. For example, you may fast social media by taking your typical social media time and interceding for people on your feed. Forfeit a meal by taking the money and donating it to a homeless shelter or soup kitchen. Fast your hobby for a month and go volunteer at a non-profit. Any of these options would put in practice this happy oracle.

Jeffrey: About a month before Jed's trip to Thailand, his host had an emergency and canceled. Jed was disappointed and confused.

He made plans to send the money back to his donors, but before he did that he knelt and prayed asking for God's will. Unbeknownst to him, somewhere in New York, a man had knelt in prayer asking God to send someone to Nepal to help him plant a church. The man, Dhan Raj, was the president of Karuna Care and was at the U.N. representing Nepal on child endangerment issues. He wanted to plant a church in the slums of Kathmandu but didn't know how to start. He had a stopover in San Francisco on his return flight and prayed that God would direct him to a church that would help him. He then typed in Google, "San Francisco Christian Church" and said, "Lord the first church that comes up I will go to and ask."

Dhan Raj showed up that Sunday. Four weeks later Jed was in Nepal, where he spent the summer planting a church, helping rescuing women from sex-trafficking, and teaching children from the Bagmati River slums. Since his first visit in 2017, Jed has returned three times to visit the church he helped plant. Today, he is a Karuna Care International board member and passionately works toward ending human trafficking in the world. He is one of the most joyfully fulfilled humans I know.

❁ Fulfillment

For Jesus, the happiness is in the hunger and thirst. In other words, there is something fulfilling in knowing our desires are right. An aligned desire itself is happy. Even before Jed arrived in Nepal and completed his mission he had already sensed a fulfillment in getting his desires aligned with God. Fulfillment is the feeling one gets when their life is aligned and their drives are focused on what is right. Fulfillment is a sense of depth and meaning anchored in an eternal weightiness.

Think of the happy feelings that ensue when we reconcile with someone who was upset with us. Think of how happy and eager we are to do right by them, and the joy we get from everything being made all right. This fulfillment is the kind of spiritual feeling our soul encounters when we are right with God and with the world.

Fulfillment is that feeling of being filled up with righteous things. Like a full tummy feels good, so does a full soul, and God wants to fill us with the divine joy of fulfillment.

❖ My Happy Declaration

I recognize God created me with hunger and thirst. I choose to direct those drives toward God. I long to be right with God and my fellow human. I now understand that my hunger to be righteous comes from God's hunger to restore. This makes me happy.

➢ Up Next: Happy are the merciful...(Matt 5:7)

Next stop, what is the triangular relationship between mercy, forgiveness and happiness? Why is mercy so hard for us to give? Is it possible to be merciful and be happy? Let's journey on!

PART III

ADVANCED

Happyluah! Congratulations on completing the second leg of your happy journey. Before you jump into the Advanced section, and if you haven't already, visit ImRealHappy.com or follow the QR code to access free supplemental resources.

CHAPTER 8

GOD'S BOOMERANG

What Goes Around Comes Around

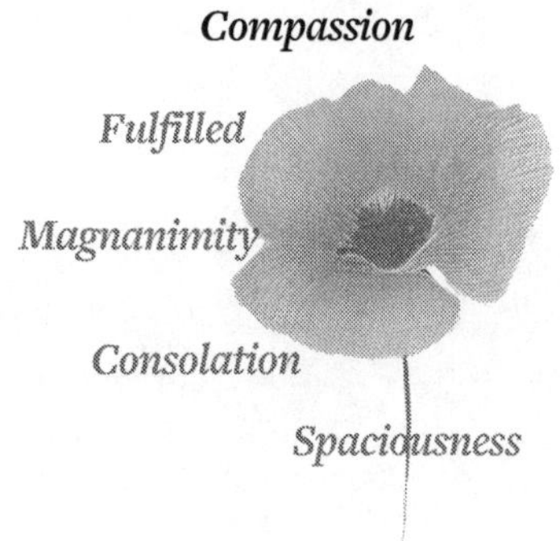

I know that each time I have acted compassionately, I have experienced a joy in me that I find in nothing else.

—Bishop Desmond Tutu

Jeffrey: I made a quick list of happy people:

Steph Curry on the sideline celebrating a teammate's three pointer,
Scotty making free breakfast sandwiches for people,
Anahit, the Armenian immigrant, passing out pizza in Golden Gate Park,
Vivian, a Puerto Rican warrior, praying for recovering addicts,
Clyde, a street performer, on Powell Street,
Deborah, teaching her life-skills class to Veterans,

My dad. He probably should be co-writing this book with Mike and not me. He is happy.

During the pandemic, he retired. He focused on his garden, his 12,000 daily steps, and his two snoring cavaliers. He watched the news hoping for something good to come of the pandemic, but news is fear-driven, crushing our hope of happiness one breaking news segment at a time. The shutdown took its toll on him, truly on all of us.

My life has paralleled much of my dad's—pastor, divorce, failures, successes, belief in God's love, and a strong second-half of life. But it's the most recent development in the golden years of his life that has me most inspired.

Our family, not unlike yours, has liberal and conservatives, republicans, democrats, and libertarians. We all love Jesus and love his teachings, but we just all see it a bit differently when it comes to politics. We never argue over politics at Christmases or Thanksgivings. I only say this so that whatever your brand of politics, you won't shut me out before I finish the story.

My dad is a Fox News watcher, my daughter more of a CNN girl, but neither judge the other. I say that because what has happened in this current season of his life is not stereotypical of a conservative who is deeply concerned with undocumented immigration issues. In the fall of 2022, his brother-in-law, Vincente, invited him to go out into the desert between Mexico and the United States to look for the dead bodies of undocumented immigrants.

"What good does that do if they are already dead?" he asked Vicente.

Vicente had launched a non-profit, Eagles of the Desert, many years ago to do this mercy work.

"If your son or daughter was dead in the desert, would you want someone to recover their body?" Vicente replied.

And that is all it took. Dad loves Kim, my sister, and me a lot.

The fourteen-mile trek through a desert isn't exactly easy for a man one year shy of eighty. He was the oldest guy out there by 30+ years and several were concerned. Some told him he was too old and others said it was too dangerous, but he didn't listen. After one desert foray, he was hooked.

Dad said, "I don't know how to describe what these desert recovery missions have done for me and how I feel. I guess I feel compassion, which I think means "suffering with" and although it doesn't sound right to say, I feel good about what I am doing better than if I just watched the news and did nothing."

As I write this chapter, he has been back four times. Last year alone this group recovered 23 dead bodies and reconnected them with their loved ones. They also rescued 215 immigrants dying in the desert. This kind of compassion is a kind of happiness the world is in desperate need of.

Last month, my dad bought a camper shell for his truck bed so he can sleep on-site. He loves it. I'm really proud of my dad for doing this.

We hope by now you realize the kind of happy we are talking about is real—it tackles real issues with real candor. We haven't avoided any subject—sadness at loss, anger at injustice, drives and appetites that run amok. Next, we come to another tough topic — mercy.

Mercy. It's a complicated topic and drawing its connection to happiness is no less simple. Mercy comes naturally in situations we deem "deserving" such as forgiving the impoverished mother who stole for food, or releasing the victim who retaliated in self-defense. However, doling out mercy becomes tricky when the wrongs trespass the boundaries of our inner judge or when we find ourselves in need of it. Mercy is further complicated by its close connection to forgiveness and compassion. Search the word mercy in a thesaurus and you are likely to find compassion and forgiveness as its synonyms. We think it's fair to say that mercy is a "loaded" word.

For many of us, our big-ticket forgiveness items—deep wounds, victimization, abuse—don't fit well with the mercy rubric. Perhaps that's why Hollywood has built an empire off revenge films. Revenge plots are littered through every genre of film—Horror, Romance, Comedy, Family, Drama, Action, even Documentaries. The quintessential revenge movie (and novel), *Count of Monte Cristo*, has been made into nineteen films alone! Revenge sells because we get to live out our revenge vicariously through these heroes.

Revenge films affirm something our base nature wants to believe—vengeance is fulfilling. We sense the imbalanced scales of justice in our world and long for stories that resolve in judicial equilibrium. And, truthfully, the thought that the unjust and the merciless go unpunished leads to a moral dissonance. We need our stories to reconcile, to see good triumph over evil.

In reality, life rarely ends like a revenge film. The credits don't roll after the coup de grâce of our nemesis. In our sequel, "Life After Vengeance," we keep on living, carrying the emotional trauma of it all, having wasted the good years of our life on perpetuating the cycles of violence. All that's left for us to do is relive over and over the moment we got even.

Is that a life worth living? Can withholding mercy tip the scales of justice into balance? Is vengeance *or* mercy the true happy antidote?

At the Heart of Happiness is . . .

> *If you want to experience the happiness of God again and again, practice mercy.*
>
> —The Beloved

Most scholars conclude that the fifth beatitude, "blessed are the merciful," is the heart of the gospel that Jesus brought to people. Below are mercy statements made by Jesus in the four gospels:

Neither do I condemn you.
Son, your sins are forgiven.
Her sins which were many, are forgiven.
Father, forgive them for they know not what they do.
Today you will be with me in Paradise.

Jesus makes mercy central to the happy oracles too. If the seven happy attitudes were ripples caused by one big splash, mercy would be the splash. Moreover, mercy is not only central to the Beatitudes, but to the whole Sermon on the Mount. What follows below is every mercy statement offered in the Sermon on the Mount.

"Be reconciled with your brother."
"Turn the other cheek."
"Love your enemies, pray for those who persecute you."
"Judge not that you be not judged."
"Forgive us our debts as we forgive our debtors."
"Forgive others their trespasses."
"How much more will your Father who is in heaven give good gifts to those who ask."
"Do unto others as you would have them do unto you."

Yes. Mercy is God's most endearing quality. Clark Pinnock, once said there is a "wideness to God's mercy" and Jesus challenges his followers to be swallowed up in its galaxious swath.[49]

Happy are the merciful for they shall have mercy shown them.

—Jesus' fifth word on happiness.

By now, you may have noticed Jesus weaves his tapestry of joy with strands of thought from the Torah, Wisdom Writings, and the Prophets. Likewise, with mercy he continues his textile of the happy life. The Sages and Psalmists proclaim repeatedly that the Creator created us by mercy, for mercy, and in mercy. The "Great Hallel," Psalm 136, riffs twenty-six times, "his mercy endures forever."[50] *The reason his mercy endures forever is because he never quits giving it away.*

> Wisdom Writing: "He who has mercy on the poor, happy *is* he..." (Proverbs 14:21, KJV)
>
> Psalms: "With the merciful you show yourself merciful" (Psalm 18:25)
>
> Prophets: "Do justice, love mercy, walk humbly before God" (Micah 6:8, KJV)

Mercy isn't a new concept for Israel; it's as old as God's mercy to the murderous Cain, the adulterous David, the fraudulent Jacob, the promiscuous Judah, the Harlot Rahab. The Torah is rife with mercy, and its pages are mercy-bound. This tender-hearted eagerness to give and forgive is the most defining attribute in God's relationship with humanity. Thus is the quintessential characteristic of God expressed in adages like, "to err is human, to forgive is divine."

Jesus' fifth word on happiness offers an image of God joyfully gifting mercy to the humble and remorseful. And in the afterglow of so much mercy, we come to believe God sees us not as a problem to be fixed, but rather as a people to be loved.

The Problem with Mercy

Mercy Means Exchange. Mercy comes from the old Etruscan word *merc*, which meant exchange. We see the root in words like mercantile, merchandise, merchant, and commerce.[51] First century merchants showed up with their goods at the city gates where villagers gathered to negotiate fair exchanges. These exchanges were transactional, ones where the business was prioritized above the relationship. Mercy is also an exchange, but it is relational, not transactional. The good or service it exchanges, which we unpack below, is forgiveness and compassion.[52]

For us to understand the process by which mercy works, we must see it as an equity. In the mercy exchange, God prioritizes the relationship above rules, rights, and fairness. As consumers of a mercy exchange, it's as if we won the emotional lottery. We celebrate, rejoice, and are grateful, clearly knowing, we are no longer indebted, relationally or otherwise. But as vendors, we fear a mercy donation will leave us emotionally bankrupted. Giving mercy requires us to pull resources from other places to cover emotional, physical, and spiritual losses. Our cultural norms and justice sensibilities are offended by the unfairness of this exchange. Hence, the problem with mercy— it violates all our definitions of justice.

Plato, in The Republic, which gives the West its view of justice, narrowed justice down to four kinds:

1. What is fair to the individual
2. What is fair to the society
3. What is fair to the cosmos (environmental context)
4. What is fair to the gods

Plato's views of justice leave no margin for mercy, and neither do ours. We prefer a transactional justice because it offers some modicum of fairness in an unfair world —if you take my eye, I take your eye (individual). If you vandalize a city park, the city punishes you (societal). If you dump nuclear waste in soil, your children and their children will suffer consequences (cosmos). The "punishment must fit the crime," as we are wont to say. Without such justice, we fear any ordered society will quickly erode. We naturally resist mercy, resent needing it, refuse to give it, and often misunderstand it as something that is weak and insipid. To show mercy in the face of transgression is unhappy, unjust, and irresponsible. In our world's market, mercy and justice just don't see eye to eye. And this is a problem for mercy.

The Merciless Heart

Truly, when we have a problem with mercy, we have a problem with God. This problem is so significant that all four Gospels record a defiant and provocative Jesus charging through the Temple courtyard, purging and overturning the merchandise and transaction tables. His strongest rebuke is reserved for the dove-sellers, the poor man's sacrifice. Somewhere between the "mercy seat" where God's presence dwelt and the entrance to the temple, the religious leaders had set up dozens of tables to exchange currency into temple coins (which they had price gouged) and animals to be sacrificed, over which they had a monopoly.

The scene misrepresents God as requiring certain transactions before he pardons and accepts people. His mercy is something we pay for, earn, or deserve by our privileged birth and status.

For years, this sacrilegious practice had gone unchallenged. Perhaps because transactional relationships are all we know and it's most natural to continue this with God.

We barter: *God, if you do ________, then I will do ________.*
We bid: *If I do ________, then God will ___________.*
We trade: *If you will me ___________ I will give you ___________.*
We demand: *I did _____________, now you must ______________.*

The haggling for mercy and clinking of money feels like an iron gate thrust between us and the entrance to God's Happy Presence. The Fourth Gospel strategically records the temple cleansing story on the heels of the first happy miracle of water to wine.[53] We just learned that God will do miracles to keep us happy, and next we learn that he will roll up his sleeves and clear a path for us to be happy with him. He wants a happy house for all people!

The religious elite get angry and plot to kill Jesus for this. Transactional extremists really don't like mercy. God was supplemental to their morality. They really didn't need God; they were too busy using God for their own profit.

Meanwhile, the crowd stands there amazed. The poor jubilantly rush in. That day people experienced God without the bouncers and ticket-checkers. Free to give, free to worship, free to love, free to be forgiven. The Psalmist prophesied this moment would come.

> *Surely his salvation is nigh them that fear him;*
> *that glory may dwell in our land.*
>
> *Mercy and truth have met together;*
> *righteousness and peace have kissed each other.*
> *(Psalm 85:9-10, KJV)*

Mercy Doesn't Mean Anything Until It Means Everything

In *Reflections on the Spiritual Intimacy of the Pastor*, a research project processing through clergy moral failure, one pastor who had lost his marriage, family, and church said, "If I had it to do all over again, I would not change anything. I never knew the mercy of God until it was all I had, and once I had it, it was everything to me."[54]

We don't know what mercy means until we need it. We

don't know how to give it until we have *had* to receive it. We are not speaking of token mercy but falling on the mercy of God. And once we have had to fall on that mercy, we encounter what Thomas Merton spoke of when he said, "mercy within mercy within mercy."[55] We tend to think that God has an outer layer of mercy, and that we have a have a one-time shot to get it right. What we come to discover is that, like nesting dolls, one mercy opens up into another mercy and another mercy. The wild nature of mercy is it's an infinite giving away of God's self to our most hideous shame.

John Newton, the eighteenth-century slave trading captain, desperately needed mercy. And when God's mercy finally saved him, he penned the sweet sounds of "Amazing Grace." There are millions of us out there who resonate with mercy meaning everything. The song is estimated to be performed on average 10 million times annually![56] Some sources suggest that "Happy Birthday" is the only song more popular.

Mercy to the inner critic. The inner critic is that self-condemning, self-criticizing, and often merciless voice. What does your inner critic say when you drop a glass or break a dish? When you fail an exam or struggle with weight loss? When you overdraft your bank account or your credit score takes a nose dive? What about when you come down with yet another ailment? When you can't quit your nicotine addiction or gossip conversations? What does your inner critic say about your body type and gender assignment?

Mercy is the exchange point where our inner critic transforms into our inner advocate. We must be willing to share this residue of God and not withhold it from any part of our life—past failures, present limitations, and future fears. Baptize the inner critic in mercy. Baptize the self-hatred, shame, the pride and anger. Mercy within mercy within mercy. Until we are full of mercy, we keep it flowing, stewarding it within every nook and cranny of our heart.

Here is the troublesome reality, our willingness to give mercy is proportional to our willingness to receive it.

Mercy to the inner judge. The inner judge is another character at work within us that is parched for mercy. That voice that levels mental and emotional micro-judgements at others. Our inner judge is about as chatty as our inner critic, jabbering away all day with decrees, pronouncements, adjudications, and final decisions at others.

The lady taking two seats on the bus, the unaccommodating airline attendant behind the counter, the man taking too long at the gas pump, and the waitress who forgot our order are all victims of our inner judge. It doesn't stop here. We *unconsciously* default to labeling, prejudice, and stereotyping.

Read through the scenes below, making note of where you sense mercy and where you sense mercilessness:

The black kid in a hoodie on a street corner. The white middle-age male in a suit in the FiDi. The elderly Asian man driving. The woman yelling at her husband. The skateboarder kid with tattoos. The man with a MAGA bumper sticker on his pickup. The woman with a coexist bumper sticker on her Volvo. The person using a government food card at Whole Foods. The parent with unruly kids. The drug addict sleeping on a sidewalk. The white family pulling into a gated community. The Californian vegan. The Texan carnivore. Elon Musk. Nancy Pelosi.

After reading that list, where you is your mercy meter tilting? Did you experience any triggers, angst, annoyance? Did you notice the absence of happiness when the inner critic or the inner judge are vociferating their opinions in your heart?

Our micro-expressions flicker with joy and kindness when our inner critic and inner judge are awash in mercy. Mercy dispatches feelings through our nervous system of patient understanding and a compassionate heart. The inner critic becomes kind and the inner judge empathetic. We aren't triggered with negativity, but feel goodness toward all humanity. And this is the kind of happiness mercy reciprocates.

Our happiness thrives when we have a constant melody of mercy humming along underneath the skin of our day! We inhale the mercy of God and exhale joyful compassion and tender understanding.

Three Steps to a Merciful Life

Trust. Jesus doesn't flinch when he says, "You have heard that it was said, 'An eye for an eye and a tooth for a tooth.' But I say to you, Do not resist the one who is evil. But if anyone slaps you on the right cheek, turn to him the other also" (Matthew 5:38-39).

With these simple words, and with his life Jesus clarifies our part in the justice equation—mercy. By giving mercy, we best support justice. These simple words require a lot of trust in God's justice. By being merciful, we are fully entrusting justice to God.

Trust is the only way to embrace mercy. Like Alyosha in Dostoyevsky's *The Brothers Karamazov,* we learn that God gives us something far greater than vengeance, far happier than a balanced ledger, and precious enough to "justify all that has happened."

> "I believe like a child that suffering will be healed and made up for, that all the humiliating absurdity of human contradictions will vanish like a pitiful mirage, like the despicable fabrication of the impotent and infinitely small Euclidean mind of man, that in the world's finale, at the moment of eternal harmony, something so precious will come to pass that it will suffice for all hearts, for the comforting of all resentments, for the atonement of all the crimes of humanity, of all the blood they've shed; that it will make it

> not only possible to forgive but to justify all that has happened."[57]

Trust starts small. Often it comes to us as a subtle inner invitation, "Hey, follow me this way, it will be okay." This invitation grows into a strong sense of knowing centered in our spirit. If we lean into it without thinking too much, we take a small step, an act of trust. The act, whether it comes from feeling or knowing or sensing, always accompanies the trust. Always.

Forgiveness. Trusting in God's mercy manifests as forgiveness first. We come to trust that forgiveness is the better way, that God will show us how, and will give us the strength. Forgiveness flows out from this trust in every direction. We forgive God. We forgive ourselves. We forgive our neighbor. In a sense, forgiveness is our first act of mercy. Like trust, it starts small, but before it's done, we are awash in an ocean of mercy and it effectively deals with the elephant in the room of our heart.

Forgiveness has a common pattern. Memoirs like those of Elizabeth Eliot, widow of martyred missionary Jim Eliot, Corrie Ten Boom, survivor of Ravensbrṳck, and Eva Kor, a survivor of Auschwitz, express similarities in the source of forgiveness, path of forgiveness and the ultimate purpose of forgiveness.

> *"Forgiveness is an act of the will, empowered by the grace of God. It is a choice to be merciful and compassionate, even in the face of great pain and injustice."—Eliot*

> *"Forgiveness is an act of love. Love is the power that forgives. God is love, and He has shown us mercy and forgiveness through His Son Jesus Christ." —Ten Boom.*

> *"Forgiveness is not so much for the perpetrator, but for the victim. It is the ultimate act of self-healing."—Kor*

Forgiveness, which is at the heart of Christianity, is a path not a feeling, an act we must walk out as part of our hero's journey. Our forgiveness journey is beyond the scope of this book. The point Jesus makes in the fifth happy oracle is that merciful people are happier. Mercy involves itself in both what is behind us (forgiveness) and what is before us (compassion). So, what is compassion?

Compassion. Rachamim is the Biblical Hebrew word for compassion, which comes from the root word for womb, *rechem*. Compassion means to "suffer with" but almost always in the sense of nurturing, caring, and in ways that are most natural to mothers. Compassion comes to us as an urge to show kindness, be selfless, and help a fellow human in need. Prophets and seers considered compassion to be the emotion of God.[58]

Forgiveness and compassion are never far from each other. They are two sides of the same mercy coin. We have observed this interplay in the remarkable, ordinary lives of people we know.

- George, by forgiving God for not healing the chronic rheumatoid arthritis in his hands, experienced God's mercy in compassion for people who suffer chronic pain. He has come to see the pain as symbolic of the spiritual pain he would have without God's mercy.
- Zoe, by forgiving her mother's neglect that led to her sexual abuse as a child, finds that the ongoing forgiveness has been the source of healing and a life mission of bringing healing to those who experienced parental neglect.

- Brandon by forgiving his father, who sabotages their relationship over and over with his untreated mental health, discovers an infinite joy of God being his ever present and wise Father
- Sharmilla who experienced God's healing mercy over her dying heart, now gives her life in the slums of Kathmandu rescuing children that are being trafficked.
- Father Leland walking San Francisco's Polk Gulch from 10pm to 4am every night praying with sex-workers, ministering to drug addicts and helping people who are overdosing.
- Tim and Karol in their sixties walking San Francisco's Tenderloin passing out hot cocoa, prayer and love.
- Johnny, with his guitar slung over his shoulder, walking into assisted living homes and elderly care facilities to lead them in sing-alongs and entertainment.
- We left one more line in the book. We believe if you got this far in the book, you should be included in it.
- ____ (that's for your name)
- ____ (that's for what mercy is doing through you)

Jesus describes his happy city, the Kingdom of God, with words like meek, pure, merciful, justice and righteousness. We are tempted to think that Jesus is asking us to demonstrate these qualities as admission into his happy city, but Jesus did not come to create another religious order. Instead, he is inviting us into a kingdom reality by painting a picture of how his citizens live and relate. He is not demanding that we mimic the culture of his city or simulate his kingdom order. Instead, he will do something so real in our hearts that mercy will flow freely down the channels of forgiveness and compassion, and before we know it, we are part of the City that Smiles.

Let's summarize the exchanges of mercy:

> First, God pours out mercy on us.
> Second, we trust this mercy and receive it.
> Third, we forgive God, ourself, our neighbor and continue this transformational journey.
> Fourth, we feel compassion and then give it away.
> Fifth, we give and receive mercy again and again... and are filled with happiness.

The Mercy Boomerang

If mercy could be purchased in a marketplace, we think it would come in the shape of a boomerang. That magical toy that we fling into the wind and watch as a few seconds later it rushes back to us. This happy oracle is the only one that returns to us again and again and again. As often as we launch it, it comes back to us. No small print limits the abundance of mercy we can garner; in fact, the more we give it, the more we get it. The mercy boomerang arcs like a heavenly smile that grins from forgiveness to compassion.

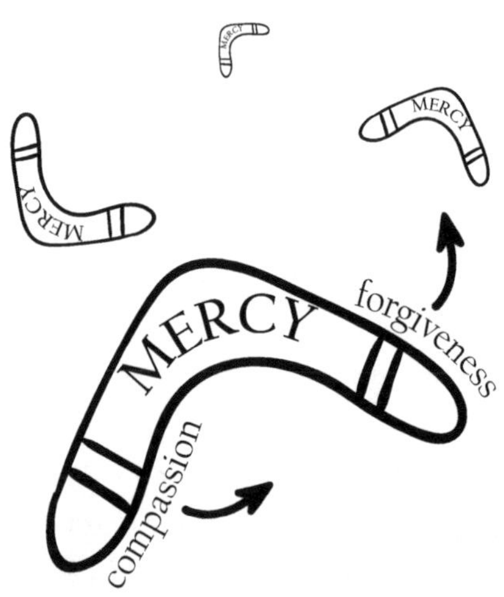

✿ Compassion

A Tibetan monk in making a case for a compassionate life said, "Look at Stalin's picture or Hitler's picture and compare it to [Desmond Tutu]. You can see that the person who has all the power, but who lacks compassion, who only thinks about control, can never be happy."[59]

We believe that mercy, when it hits our feeling center, gurgles up as the happy emotion of compassion, making it not just something we do, but also feel. Jewish and Christian scholars have long held that compassion is the very emotion of God.[60] When humans feel it, they act courageously, almost without thinking; the emotion overpowers self-preservation, fear, doubt, or anger. The result is a joyful sense of God's emotions flooding the heart with a deep sense of solidarity with someone in need of mercy.

Jeffrey: Eagles of the Desert, the rescue and body recovery non-profit, was started by a man in his sixties that saw in the news how vigilantes were shooting immigrants near the California border. After three of these fatal shootings, he decided to had to do something. He wanted to work with and not against the border patrol but in a humanitarian capacity. He started by replacing the water jugs that the vigilantes had riddled with holes. After getting permission and heading out, he realized that the greater need wasn't water but recovery of bodies. He armed himself with crosses, headed out, and planted crosses near the bodies he found. He then organized teams to recover the bodies and notify the family back home. Before he knew it, his Facebook page was inundated with mother's and father's tearful requests for help. And thus, his little army of compassionate desert eagles was born.

Much like the Grinch who stole Christmas, we smile wide when we feel our hearts expand in compassion, when all at once we realize we have a senseless capacity for it. We feel joy when our hearts are freed to give mercy upon mercy upon mercy. And that joy, as it morphs into works of kindness and acts of compassion, comes back like a boomerang again and again in the mercy exchange. Mercy is a lasting and returning joy.

❖ My Happy Declaration

I understand that mercy is an exchange. God watches over my offerings of mercy and rewards me again and again. Out of God's mercy, flows forgiveness and compassion. As I receive mercy, and give forgiveness and show compassion, my life is filled with real happiness.

➢ Up Next: Happy are the pure in heart... (Matt 5:8)

In the next happy oracle Jesus points out that unhappiness can be a vision problem. Many lament our search for happiness with the words "we still haven't found what we're looking for." Next, we will learn how to clear our field of vision to behold the happiness right under our nose.

CHAPTER 9

"100%!!!"

Seeing The Happiness That Is All Around

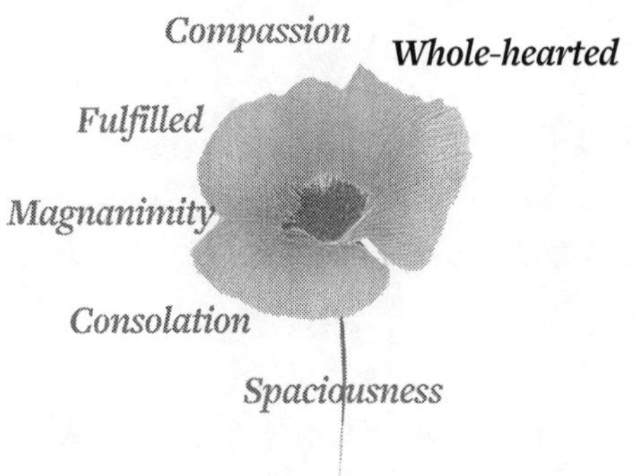

The real voyage of discovery consists not in seeking new landscapes but in having new eyes.
—Marcel Proust

Mike: When speaking of "the pure in heart," I've known such a man.

My own dad, Jimmy Burdett Hayes, who has entered the City that Smiles, was that man. Dad was not raised in church, or trained in the Scripture, but was an obedient child. He joined the Navy during WW2 and returned to marry his sweetheart, Shirley, my mom. When I was about two years old, they followed their hunger for meaning and both became Christians. Eventually, dad went on to become a pastor and plant a church in Flagstaff, Arizona.

Dad was a positive man, and by that I mean it was like he added a positive sign (+) on all his conversations, activities, and body language.

An "A" was always an A+! I never once saw him angry or out of control. Dad loved my mom and seemed to get great joy out of making her laugh. Now, he wasn't a deep thinker, but he was a pure-hearted encourager with pure-hearted laughter.

At about age seventy-eight, Dad developed dementia. His mind slowly decreased in function. Then Parkinson's set in, the kind that stiffens the body. A man who had only known a life of health and lived by faith became a man fighting for his life on multiple fronts.

As a pastor, he loved to pray for those who were sick or troubled. He saw God when he prayed for people, and I suppose it was because he did it with such purity of heart. In my lifetime, I witnessed countless miracles when Dad prayed. As I reflect, it reminds me of Jesus saying, "I can do nothing but what I see my Father do."

Dad needed his own miracle now, and we earnestly prayed for him, but he seemed more preoccupied with stewarding his spirit and attitude than with his physical health.

Do you remember the character Kramer in Seinfeld? You know how he always entered a room by bursting through the door and sliding to a stop? In those later years, dad's upbeat and joyful positivity was a lot like Kramer bursting through a door.

One day, my sister, Jenny, took Dad to his doctor visit. We all were concerned about how the disease was progressing. When he returned, he flung the door open, threw his arms up in the air and grinning from ear-to-ear announced, "Doctor said I'm 100%!!!!"

He maintained that "100%" report after each doctor visit or phone call with medical staff. His hands in the air, his positivity intact, and making sure our concerns were alleviated. Dementia and Parkinson's eventually took dad's life, but they never took his joy. He was happy until the end. For dad, a pure heart meant he found joy in everything. And he did. He practiced this "100%" and it was through this "100%" that he saw God.

Have you ever found yourself searching for your keys, wallet, or phone? You drive back to the restaurant, rummage through the garage, and mentally retrace all your steps. The longer you look, the more frustrated, worried, and anxious you get. Should you cancel the bank cards and phone account? And then, suddenly out of thin air, your lost item appears on the kitchen counter. It was right under your nose the whole time! How is it possible to look right at it and not see it?! It's a frustrating experience to be within eyeshot of the thing you're searching for but unable to see.

This experience is a compelling metaphor for our pursuit of happiness. Just like searching for our lost belongings, we retrace our steps to the last time we were happy. Can we ever recover the happiness that got lost along the way? What if we have lost happiness once and for all?

But what if we told you that what we are looking for isn't really lost, stolen, or dead? What if the key to pursuing happiness is perceiving happiness? What if happiness is right under our nose, literally, in our heart?

Happiness, Hidden in Plain Sight

> *"The best and most beautiful things in the world cannot be seen or even touched. They must be felt with the heart."*
>
> *—Helen Keller*

News spreads that Jesus was headed back to the hillside. Months have passed since the famous Sermon on the Mount. Merchants close shop, moms wrap up their domestic work, and grab the kids. Groups of farmers and artisans make their way to the spot Jesus is rumored to be. Debates and animated conversations carry each group along. *What happy oracle might he wow them with today?* The crowd builds to five thousand happy-eyed men, plus women and children, all waiting with bated breath for the next life-giving, soul-freeing word of the day.

Also in attendance are a delegation of Jerusalem's Pharisees and Scribes. The two religious sects appear in tandem throughout the happy Rabbi's good news tour to scrutinize him and remind the people of their authority and reach.

Pharisees were religious reformers who sought to renew Israel to holiness through the moral code of Torah law, of which there were more than 613! They worked with Scribes, first century lawyers, not much different from a lawyer today. The Torah was their constitution and case law. They tried their cases from small claims courts up through Jerusalem's Supreme Court.

Together, the Pharisees and Scribes were building a case against Jesus. So far, their case file included: guilt by association (eating with sinners), conspiracy to commit fraud (casting out demons by the power of Satan), and violation of Torah labor laws (picking grain on the Sabbath). Today, they hoped to add a violation report of moral or religious codes to their file. Jesus' broad disregard for the established purity guidelines and unsanctioned assembly were disconcerting to the establishment. Furthermore, the critical mass of Jesus' growing crowds needed to be quelled before it reached a tipping point and social control was lost.

By now you have probably guessed we are at the scene of the miracle of feeding the five thousand. This wilderness lunch was a big deal. It's the only miracle that made the final cut into all four Gospels. And this meal, the size of the crowd seated in a desolate wilderness faint with hunger, echoed Moses and his wilderness manna. Meals were symbols of friendship, rest and hospitality. There was a lot of laughter and miracle-hope that day. The smell of fresh bread, the saltiness of smoked fish, and the animated buzz of voices set the stage for the kind of grassroots movement that the Pharisees and Scribes needed to nip in the bud.

Conservative estimates would say that fifteen thousand people were fed that day! And yet, immediately following the wonder-filled wilderness brunch, the legal team investigates Jesus and his disciples for their failure to wash before eating (violation of purity-health code).[61]

Why couldn't the Scribes and Pharisees celebrate the all-you-can-eat buffet for what it was? Hungry people being fed. Why couldn't they participate with their hungry countrymen, as an undeniable, taste-it-in-your-mouth miracle? Or why couldn't they, as theologians, rejoice in a God who sees their national hunger in the face of heavy Roman taxation, and be affirmed by this miracle?

While the peasants were eating the best meal of their lives, the killjoys investigated the improprieties of unwashed hands. Their blind response to the situation begs the question, *how is it that some come to see God while others can look right at him and miss him?* How is it that the epic alabaster box-breaking moment got turned into a disgruntled debate about "waste" and conservation? (John 12:1-8) Jesus could see the prophetic significance, why couldn't Judas? And while God freed a girl from human trafficking, the hapless sat around and bastardized her character (Luke 7:36-50). What's wrong with us? Why can't we see God in these beautiful moments? And why do we feel good about making others feel bad?

Jesus responds to the party poopers with bold words and insightful words.

"It's not what you swallow that pollutes your life, but what you vomit up...what comes out of the mouth gets its start in the heart. It's from the heart that we vomit up evil arguments, murders, adulteries, fornications, thefts, lies...That's what pollutes" (Matthew 15:16-20, MSG).

Jesus' word to all of us: unhappiness is a condition of an

impure heart. Missing the happiness in a joyful wilderness banquet is a heart problem. Not being able to see God in the communal joy and laughter of a miracle lunch is heart blindness.

We need, in the most urgent kind of way, purified hearts. We need hearts unbiased by power, greed, and jealousy. If Jesus is right and happiness is proportional to our purity of heart, what chance do we have of seeing God? Surely only a handful of people could ever attain that kind of cleanliness.

In his next happy oracle, Jesus is keen to locate happiness in the heart, and when we go searching for happiness by looking inside, rather than outside ourselves, we will find it.

> *Happy are the pure in heart, for they shall see God.*
>
> —Jesus' sixth word on happiness.

In *Happiness: A History,* Darrin McMahon takes readers through the first 500 years of history's pursuit of happiness showing how enticing, yet exclusive and ultimately elusive happiness was for the Mediterranean world. For Socrates, Plato, and Aristotle happiness was "a godlike life" beyond the reach of mere mortals. Just before introducing the readers to Jesus' happy life McMahon says, "they searched for happiness where they could until it was found—re-found—in the face of God."[62] In other words the philosophers merely had conversations about happiness from one century to the next, but Jesus' arrival offered the countenance of happiness.

If antiquity's pursuit of happiness concluded that it was found and re-found in the face of God, why are we looking elsewhere?

To start, in all cultures and mythologies, the gods were not something to be sought. They were to be avoided and feared rather than faced and enjoyed. From the Epic of Gilgamesh (circa 2100 BC) to the Fall of Icarus (8 CE), man's encounter with the gods was anything but happy. Even the God of the Jewish Scriptures said to Moses, "you cannot see my face, for man shall not see me and live" (Exodus 33:20). Our fear of God is anthropological. Every biblical encounter with God begins with the same words: "Fear not!"

Abraham when he had a vision of God (Genesis 15:1)
Hagar when she encountered the Angel of God (Genesis 21:17)
Daniel when he had a vision of God (Daniel 10:12)
Isaiah when he saw the glory of the Lord (Isaiah 6:5)

We have been pre-conditioned to be terrified of God, not happified by God. Perhaps now we can understand what C. S. Lewis meant when he said, "It is safe to tell the pure in heart that they shall see God, for only the pure in heart want to."[63] When we open the pages of the Christian Scriptures, we find one story after another of people coming face-to-face with God and returning happy.

The angel announces to the pure-in-heart Virgin Mary, "Do not be afraid!" In the radiant light of that vision, she pens the Magnificat, a song where she declares herself the *most happy* (*makarios*) of all generations. But an interesting experiential shift occurs from Jesus' birth forward. The customary "fear not" seems rendered obsolete, and those who come to behold the face of God in Jesus experience happiness, not fear. Simeon peers into the infant Jesus and declares, "Nunc Dimittis" (I can now die happily). Simon Peter recognizes Jesus as the face of God and declares, "You are the Son of the Living God!" And Jesus replies, "Happy *(makarios)* are you, Simon!" (Matthew 16:17)

There were many elders walking through the Temple the day that Simeon saw God in the face of the infant Jesus. Others roving about missed the God-sighting. There were many crowds following Jesus, looking for and seeing a rabbi, but only Simon saw God in Jesus. This is a frequent motif in Scripture. Daniel's companions flee and miss the angelic vision. Saul's Damascus Road companions hear a sound but see nothing, while Saul sees Jesus. How is it that God can be right under our nose, and we miss him?

Pure Means Cleansed

Before we take our etymological dive into the word pure, let's clear the path by clarifying what pure is NOT. Jesus does not say, "Blessed are the blameless and mistake-free lives." Who could see God if perfection was the qualifying standard for divine sight? Rather, Jesus speaks about a condition of heart. Thank goodness! God sees our heart; our heart sees God. And the words 'pure heart' are the clue to that happy way of seeing.

Pure hearts are cleared of anything that obscures the path to a vision of God. Which brings us to the question: what did Jesus mean when he used the word pure?

Katharos, from which we derive our word catharsis, is the Greek word for pure. A cathartic moment usually refers to the kind of crying that cleanses us, where we come to see things clearly. *Katharos* is also the kind of cleansing that happens to a precious metal. Gold ore mined from the earth is mixed with iron, lead, quartz, and other minerals. It is only pure gold after it is *cleansed.* Likewise, an impure heart is cloudy, murky, and smoggy. For example, when we are jealous, we cannot see anything but the thing someone else possesses. When we are mucked up with self-pity, our negative feelings blind us to real and present blessings. Impure hearts only want to see what is wrong and why things are so bad. Impure hearts need *katharos.*

Pure Means Single

> *Final and perfect happiness can consist in nothing else than the vision of the Divine Essence. To make this clear, two points must be observed.*

> *First, that man is not perfectly happy, so long as something remains for him to desire and seek: secondly, that the perfection of any power is determined by the nature of its object.*
>
> —Thomas Aquinas

We took the above quote from Aquinas' *Summa Theologica*, where the great philosopher critiques the "things in which man's happiness consists:" wealth, honor, fame, power, beauty and pleasure. After reasoning through his own objections to each, he concludes that a single-focused vision of God is the only source of perfect happiness.[64]

Similarly, Jesus, in the same beatitude discourse, connects the idea of a single vision to happy enlightenment when he says, "If your eye is single, your whole body is full of light" (Matthew 6:22, NET). Jesus reminds his followers that those who are distracted with several masters, idols, and visions are anxious.

Our eyes are constantly roving about looking for things that can give ultimate happiness. This becomes a problem for our happy sensibilities because once we have selected the objects of our ultimate happiness, we give our attention and energy to them. Before long, we are obsessed, preoccupied and unconsciously worshipping all our happy idols.

The 1930's song, *I Only Have Eyes For You,* gets at the undistracted singleness of vision Aquinas and Jesus have in mind:

> You are here and so am I
> Maybe millions of people go by
> But they all disappear from view
> And I only have eyes for you—

All the idolatrous distractions fade into the periphery when our heart is one love with God. This way of sacramental seeing beholds God everywhere.

The Sacrament of Sight

Judaism was aniconic—without idols. The only image of God was the woman and man—the image-bearers. Idols were impure images of the divine, and for this reason, words became the medium by which God was mediated. Words, like Hebrew Scriptures, came about through prophets who saw God in visions, dreams, and encounters and chronicled their experiences. God wanted the world to see his image in his children, not in a totem pole or talisman.

The most explicit example we have of words as a medium for God is Moses ascending the 'mount of God' and receiving the Ten Commandments directly from the finger of God. God used words to communicate who God was, what God was like, and how to bear God's image. With these words, Israel learned how each part of their humanity could purely reflect the holy God and how to see God.[65]

Commandments (Exodus 20:1-17)

1. God is holy. *have no other gods.*
2. Worship is holy. *have no graven image.*
3. Prayer is holy. *do not take God's name in vain.*
4. Time is holy. *Remember the Sabbath.*
5. Family is holy. *Honor mother and father.*
6. Life is holy. *Do not murder.*
7. Sex is holy. *Do not commit adultery.*
8. Matter is holy. *Do not steal.*
9. Language is holy. *Do not bear false witness.*
10. Neighbors are holy. *Do not covet.*

While Moses was receiving these words, Israel was dancing around a golden calf. Implied in this moment, is the truth that we will never see God in our objects of affection, but we see God reflected in each other's lives.

The words and image of God came together in Jesus, the image of the invisible God.[66] He is all about reflecting God to us, and he comes showing us how to be pure and happy image bearers. As he ascends the Mount of Happy Attitudes with his merry band of followers he adds, "the heart is holy, and when its holy it's also happy."

Jesus pulls all these ideas together from the twenty-fourth Psalm (v.4-6), which maps out the ascent to seeing the face of God with the following waypoints: clean hands, pure heart, blessedness (*ashrei*, the Hebrew word for happy).

> Who shall *ascend the hill of the Lord*? And who shall stand in his holy place?
> He who has *clean* hands and *a pure heart*, who does not lift up his soul to what is false and does not swear deceitfully.
> He will receive *blessing* from the Lord and righteousness from the God of his salvation.
> Such is the generation of those who seek him, *who seek the face of the God of Jacob.*[67]

Thomas Aquinas, as a young man felt called to give himself to knowing God. He wholeheartedly pursued this calling, refusing his family's privileged life of nobility and even the church's prestigious abbot position. All he wanted was to seek God, and he gave his life to this pursuit.

Aquinas's intellect was so prodigious, and his passion for understanding God's writings so great, that it took five scribes working in shifts just to keep up with his output. His greatest work, Summa Theologica, is a massive tome that spans over 3,500 pages. Interestingly, the book comes to an abrupt stop almost mid-sentence in a discussion on sacraments and purification.

Shortly thereafter, on December 6, 1273, as the forty-nine-year-old Aquinas received Communion at an Advent service, he was transfixed by a vision of God. This mystical experience, transcending words, and bursting with ineffable beauty, engulfed him in such wholehearted ecstasy that everything halted, rendering even his pen immobile. Despite Reginald of Piperno, his disciple, imploring him to complete his theological treatise, Thomas remained silent. Days later, as Reginald persisted, Thomas uttered these final words, "I've had an experience of God. Everything I have written is mere straw. I will never write another word."

A mere four months later, he peacefully passed away.

Aquinas shows us that words help us process and purify our hearts, but even words halt in the vision of God. We need them to grapple with seeing an invisible God. The Summa Theologica leaves no stone unturned as it fastidiously pursues God. It argues back and forth, taking one side then another. But then, as Thomas Aquinas encounters the presence of God and sees the beatific vision, the words stop. Everything is simple, even to the point that he considers his work "straw." It's interesting that he was writing on purification and receiving the sacraments when he sees God and is so transfixed by this beauty that he refuses to write another word.

The Path to a Pure Heart

Dante's Divine Comedy throws most of us off. There is nothing funny or humorous about meandering through the nine circles of Hell or scaling the nine strata of Purgatorio. However, Greek Classics, which Dante canonizes, catalogue stories with bad endings as Greek Tragedies and happy endings as Greek Comedies. While Dante's story opens in a tragic wilderness, it beautifully ends in a cosmic vision of God as "the Love that moves the Sun and other stars."[68]

The Beatific Vision, however, requires a not so comedic quest. Dante, intent on bringing us along, cries for someone to guide us. Three sages respond. The first guides us through nine intensifying circles of the Inferno and then up the nine terraces of Mount Purgatorio. Each circle and terrace afford an opportunity to purify our heart.

We finally emerge and are met by the second guide who leads us through the ten heavens of Paradise, where we continue to purify, until the final guide meets us, the one who will usher us into our vision of God. It is through a pure heart that we come to know "the entire universe [is] smiling . . . O endless joy. O ineffable happiness. O perfect life of Love and Peace."[69]

The three sages are allegorical metaphors for how we complete the pilgrimage to a pure heart.

1. *Self-examination.* Virgil, the Roman pastoral poet, leads us to self-examination and personal growth. From him we learn that only purification can usher us out of the Inferno and beyond Mt. Purgatorio. The purification brought on by self-examination sets us on the path to our vision of God.
2. *Discernment.* Beatrice, an embodiment of heavenly wisdom, meets us upon our arrival to Paradise. Her concern is purifying our understanding of love and faith. She is the Sophia, the wisdom of God, and she readies us to see God by discipling us to intimately know God.
3. *Contemplative Prayer.* Finally, Bernard of Clairvaux arrives to guide us into the heavenly vision. He leads us into contemplative prayer and oneness with God. He shows us how to "look up" and become "more and more purified [and] see deeper and deeper into the One True Light . . . the Infinite Goodness . . . until [we are] completely consumed."

To be sure, the first part of Dante's quest for happiness is by far the most difficult leg of his journey. Nine Hells and Purgatorio symbolize Dante's heart purification process, after which he is conditioned to see (through discernment) and readied to walk out the remainder of his quest into union with God.

In our impurity, we are naturally predisposed to self-loath, self-justify, and self-absorb. We opt to neglect self-examination and dismiss introspection, where the purification process begins. But the moment we orient ourselves toward self-examination—*What is it in me that makes me unhappy? What does my soul really want? Where can I grow? If I could make one life choice, right now, to set myself on the path to future happiness, what would it be?*—we begin our existential exit from the hells that hold us.

Self-examination usually leads to holy sorrow and then into supplication. Supplication is a fervent kind of prayer that combines self-reflection and repentance in earnest to God; and there is no substitute for this kind of cathartic prayer. Jacob supplicates with God for the face-to-face blessing and is blessed. David journals his supplication for a pure heart and rejoices in "the joy of salvation." Jesus supplicates in Gethsemane as a way to prepare his heart for his crucifixion and return to the Father.

To help us, the Psalter provides a wealth of literature on this subject. Supplicate with a psalm and you'll see what we mean. We have provided several categories suited to different distractions of the heart.

- Psalm 24 when you want to ascend the mountain and see the face of God.
- Psalm 4 when your eyes are distracted by the negativity of those around you.
- Psalm 5 when you're distracted by cheating or lying.
- Psalm 8 when you have the vision and don't want to lose sight of God.
- Psalm 23 when you are distracted by anxiety or even the nearness of death.
- Psalm 27 when fear distracts you.

- Psalm 37 when financial struggles distract you.
- Psalm 46 when the news and media distract you.
- Psalm 51 when your failures and sins distract you.
- Psalm 73 when your envy distracts you.
- Psalm 139 when loneliness distracts you.
- Psalm 145 when you're blinded by negativity.

The patient work of purification transforms our resentments into gratitude, hostility into hospitality, and jealousy into compersion. This all takes time, hence the nine circles of hell and nine strata mountain. There are no shortcuts along the way of self-examination. There is no way to purification but through and up, but the glorious vision of God, the trade out for a heart that sees, it's like finally walking in heaven on earth where the gate of heaven is everywhere, and like Paul, the scales have fallen from our eyes and we are given hearts to see.

'Til We Have Faces

The Hebrew Scriptures share a beautiful picture: Moses ascending into the clouds of the mountain of God. Once he arrives in God's presence, he removes a veil uncovering any fakery or façade. He stands, a mere mortal before his God. C. S. Lewis's final and favorite work of fiction, *Till We Have Faces,* offers a peek into the glory of beholding God. Lewis retells the Greek myth of the beautiful Psyche, but from the perspective of her sister Orual. Orual's quest, captured by the title, can also be framed as her central question: "How can [the Divine] meet us face to face till we have faces?"[70]

Orual acknowledges she cannot see the Divine with the "babble" of false beliefs, misconceptions, or self-deception. She must remove her veil and come to the truth, which is to know both her true self as well as believe in her true Lord.

Lewis captivates us with the arduous internal journey to recover our true face through a purified heart. At the heart of the story lies a divine, invisible castle. Her sister, Psyche, sacrifices everything for this castle. Orual, however, sees the castle, but refuses to trust her eyes. Much like our Pharisees and Scribes who see the wilderness miracle, but are jealous, selfish and demand answers and proofs, Orual does the same. It's only in her elderly years and after much self-reflection that her heart opens— her doubts, jealousies, and tainted perceptions are transformed. With her veil removed and her true heart revealed, Orual peers into a watery pool. The waters remind us of the gloating Narcissus, but what Orual sees is unimaginably glorious. In her reflection she sees three truths. That day in the waters Orual sees her sister Psyche and the Lord reflected in her true and beautiful self. No longer does she see God through doubt and fear, or her sister through eyes of jealousy or greed. At last, Orual sees through the eyes of a purified heart. And at last she has true sight, the kind of seeing that renders a pure reflection of our true self, of God and of others. Her final narration reminds us that the answers we are searching for are not reductions of words and concepts but:

> *I know now, Lord, why you utter no answer. You are yourself the answer. Before your face questions die away. What other answer would suffice? Only words, words; to be led out to battle against other words. Long did I hate you, long did I fear you. I might—*[71]

Lewis brilliantly ends the book right there. In the face of God, words are no longer meaningful and the halo around our countenance is the glow of happiness. With pure hearts we finally see the truest part of others and our truest selves in the light of God. And until that transformative moment we are fated to create images of God, others and ourselves, false idols and false selves; we remain hidden behind veils of envy, arrogance, and resentment. The joy and happiness of a pure heart is that it both reveals God to us, us to each other, and us to our true selves.

✿ Wholehearted

God's eye-to-eye encounters are heart-to-heart moments. Once we see God, we see nothing else. We want nothing else. We finally see God is everywhere and everything to us. We feel a singleness with God! Nature. People. Kindness. Grief. Worship. Work. What we are feeling and experiencing is wholeheartedness. This wholehearted happiness is a way of seeing with our feeling. Meister Eckhart, the thirteenth century Christian mystic said, "The eye through which I see God is the same eye through which God sees me; my eye and God's eye are one eye, one seeing, one knowing, one love."[72] We feel gleefully whole-hearted as we happily bear God's image and see God in it all.

❖ My Happy Declaration

I deeply long to see God. I purify my heart through self-examination, singleness of focus, and supplication. Today I begin to see God everywhere and will be bathed in happiness.

➢ Up Next: Happy are the Peacmakers... (Matt 5:9)

At the start of our journey, we suggested the happy attitudes are sequential. This is no more clearly seen than when we navigate into our next topic: peace-making. Why is this topic left toward the end of the happy manifesto? Well, if you got this far, you know that the happiness growing inside of you is something the world needs, and the next oracle helps us happify the world.

CHAPTER 10

THE HAPPY MAKERS

Getting Our World Right

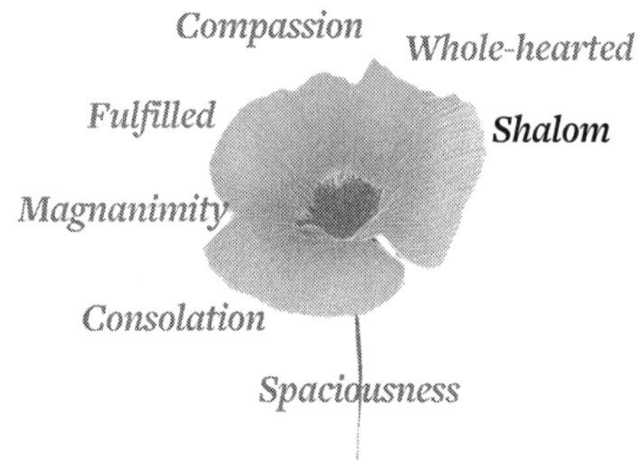

We are not at peace with others because we are not at peace with ourselves, and we are not at peace with ourselves because we are not at peace with God.

—Thomas Merton

Mike: In August 2017, I traveled to Irbil, Iraq on a peacemaking mission. I was accompanied by my son, Stephen, and we met there with a small delegation from the United States. Our mission was to meet with the Kurdish leadership about their desire to have their own homeland. We found the Kurdish leaders to be warm and welcoming. The Kurds have desired an official homeland that respects the boundaries they have enjoyed for thousands of years. Their ethnic identity has a rich history known back in Biblical times as the Medes.

The Peshmerga, Kurdish special forces, escorted us in black Suburbans to our peacemaking meetings. The streets of Irbil were fraught with dangerous roving militias. As we rushed through the street, it began to occur to me that peacemaking is much more difficult than peacekeeping.

The plight of the Kurds is a difficult one. At the end of WWI in 1916, Britain and France, with an agreement from Russia, secretly drew out national boundaries that excluded the Kurds. The Asia Minor Agreement established what is modern day Iraq, Iran and Turkey. The boundaries were drawn in such a way that the homeland of the Kurds was parceled out to Turkey, Iran and Iraq, leaving them without a country. They don't have a national boundary, and they haven't been allowed to establish their own official government and homeland. Through the years, we had supported several humanitarian projects in the region, during which times I was informed of their plight and their desired location where Syria, Iran, Turkey and Iraq share a border.

This trip in 2017 was different. It wasn't just humanitarian work but there was potential for political work to be done. Several of us with access to the White House were cautiously hopeful of getting a peaceful solution to a homeland for the Kurds. The Kurds rolled out the best of Mediterranean in hopes that the White House might guide them in establishing their own country.

While I was meeting with the Kurdish leaders, I felt a special bond with the head leader of the Kurds. He exuded a peace and patient wisdom. At the end of the third day, he noticed a lapel pin that I wore for our Center for National Renewal in Washington DC. He asked if I had one for him. As I pinned it on his lapel, it occurred to me how he wanted to represent us just as we were representing him. He proudly and eagerly wore our pin. We now had something in common, a shared symbol. Both of us stood there with pins saying, Center for National Renewal, the pin meant something more than what I had ever envisioned. I could see in his eyes the longing for the renewal of his people. In this sense, we were very much alike, very much connected in our human longing for peace and peacefulness in the world.

As the White House thought through issues with oil and military bases, they took the position that it would not benefit the White House to spend political capital advocating for the Kurds. Additionally, Turkey, Iraq, and Iran would not benefit from giving the Kurds their own land. Three countries would have had to reduce their size and alter their border boundaries to make real peace with the Kurds and another expend its political capital. Making peace for the Kurds —giving them a national homeland—would cost too much for everyone. In the end, national self-interest stood in the way of making peace for a people who have waited so long for it. So, the powers that be opted for peacekeeping instead.

We, the citizens of the world, do desperately want peace, but not always at our expense. Sadly, yet often, we find it easier to keep peace with "peace talks" or by enforcing peace with big guns and military oversight versus making real peace by opening our hearts and demonstrating faith. As I pondered the difference between peacekeeping and peacemaking, I realized how the world pats itself on the back when it keeps the peace. Jesus says, "We can do better, we can make peace."

In the opening pages of the first book of western history, Herodotus lays out how humans are on a quest for happiness. Within a few years, "the awful outcome of the search for human happiness" has resulted in a nearly 100-year war between Persia and Greece.[73] Our constant quest for happiness has resulted in violence and war throughout human history, which to state the obvious, has led us to anything but happiness.

Alfred Nobel, a Swedish Lutheran, invented dynamite in 1867. His patent not only brought him great fortune but also criticism for its mass destruction in warfare. The criticism was so harsh that, allegedly, a French newspaper in 1888 prematurely published his obituary with the heading, "The Merchant of Death is Dead." Whether it was this epitaph or his brother's death during the invention process, Alfred was so distraught over how dynamite was used in warfare that he confided in a friend, "I want to be remembered for peace, not destruction." He decided to use his fortune to promote peace and the use of knowledge for good. In his will, which he signed in 1895, he left 94% of his estate to establish the Nobel Prizes. The prizes were to be awarded annually in recognition of outstanding achievements in the service of humanity. The fields of physics, chemistry, medicine, literature and, ultimately peace were chosen as the categories. Nobel specified that the peace prize should be awarded to the person who had done the most to promote peace in the world. He wanted to motivate and inspire others to seek peace, to pursue peace, and to make peace. Nobel realized that happiness was in grave jeopardy if each person simply sought their own individual happiness and not the happiness of the world.[74]

The selfish quest for happiness occasionally results in loss, brokenness, and even when we succeed, there are hurtful outcomes. For most of us, it's not at the level of dynamite but on the level of home, work, and community. Things are thought, then said, then done and eventually bridges erode, become unsafe, and are finally burned. The messiness and ugliness we feel throughout the demolition of what was once peaceful and fun collapses into loneliness and isolation. Some researchers claim this is the main cause for unhappiness in our world today. The inability to embrace diversity, differences, and disagreements with a healthy and mature perspective leads to the persistent drama in our world.

Think about a time when you were politically divisive, theologically argumentative, ideologically harsh, or engaged in cultural warring with someone. Where would you rank your joy meter? Immediately afterwards did you feel meek, pure-in-heart, merciful? Or did you feel vindictive, proud, and hateful? This is not the life-giving joy Jesus had in mind. While healthy, lively, disagreements can exist and even feel life-giving, most of our disagreements result in fear, anger, and relational exile.

The single consistent conclusion in virtually every research project on happiness is that happiness is shared with others—family, community, neighbors. This sharing involves giving and taking, understanding and learning, humility and respect, and most of all love. When we are estranged from those we love, or are lonely and without love, our happiness eventually dries up. Without a happy outflow, it doesn't matter how much happy inflow we have, we will be like the Dead Sea, a body of water without a happy river running through it. This doesn't mean that everybody needs the same level of social interaction, but happiness thrives when it participates in the happiness of others.

In this chapter, we take on getting our relationships right and our world right. We are hopeful that even if we cannot get our world right, we can get ourselves right with the world. Afterall, that seems to be what Jesus is after in this next word on happiness.

> *Happy are the peacemakers for they shall be called children of God.*
>
> —Jesus' seventh word on happiness.

By now, we are accustomed to Jesus' artistic palette of the Wisdom Books and the Prophets from which he mixes hues of happiness with tones and shades of prophetic longing. Here, Jesus sketches from the folksy Proverbs, "those who promote peace have joy" and his words warm us like a Sieger Koder painting.

When we step back from these words and take in the vast landscape on which they are painted, we see happiness has a flow. This stream of thought came through the deep blue waters of meekness, and white rapids of righteousness, the cool turquoise pools of mercy and pure-heartedness, and now naturally we arrive at headways of peace. Here in these waters, a concentric ripple effect makes peace flow in growing circles outward to the world.

For Jesus' audience, hearing about happy peacemaking as it echoed off the walls of centuries of a Babylonian captivity, Ptolemy temple desecration, and now Roman taxation may have, and understandably so, excited some consternation. Do we get peace through conquest? Do we get peace through re-seizing what is rightfully ours? Do we make peace with each other but keep our enemies at a distant place of distrust? Jesus wasn't the first prophet to challenge the oppressed Jews to make peace of their situation.

Babylonian Shalom

The Jerusalem of Jeremiah's day was ransacked by the invading Babylonians. Then in a move to demoralize and rip all hope out of the nation of Judah, the Babylonians exiled the children and professional class a thousand miles from home. Babylon repeated this destructive deportation two more times until Jerusalem was a heap of rubble and vacant.

The prophet Jeremiah urged Judah to see the exile as a time of learning and growing. He told them that inner happiness could not be taken hostage by outer circumstances and directed them in how to live happily even in exile. The key was through one of the richest Hebrew words, *shalom*: peace.

Shalom is layered with the rich textures of shared prosperity, communal wellbeing and communal joy. In short, it is communal and social happiness.

And it was this word Jeremiah strategically reinforced in his instructions on living happily in exile. He wrote, when you arrive in Babylon, "...work for the shalom and prosperity of Babylon, pray for the shalom of Babylon, for in the happiness of Babylon will be your happiness." (Jeremiah 29:7a, PT). Shalom, then, is being a good citizen, settling in and building houses, planting gardens, growing families and launching businesses, all with the intent of making Babylon a better place. The prophetic call challenged them to live everyday life with the intent of prospering others, even their captors and enemies.

Shalom means we seek the happiness of others, we seek to make others happy. The clue to where happiness will be recovered is in the final words, "for in its shalom you will find your shalom."(Jeremiah 29:7b, PT) That is, when you bring shalom to your captors, you bring shalom to your family.

Pax Romana

Persia eventually overtakes Babylon. After a total exile of seventy years, the Persian King allowed the Jews to return home, yet little changed by way of freedom or national autonomy. For the first few years, the Persians taxed them, followed by the Greeks, then the Ptolemies and finally Rome. Each empire had its version of oppression and Rome's came packed as the Pax Romana: Roman peace.

In contrast to Jesus' shalom, Rome achieved its peace through intimidation, cruelty, and heavy taxation meant to support the militant "peace-keepers." Not far from where Jesus sat giving his seventh oracle, the General Varus, a few decades earlier, marched through and lined the road from Sepphoris to Galilee with two thousand crucified Jewish rebels. The Galilean's powerlessness took their happiness hostage. As a result, the growing sentiment in the Galilee was that peace and happiness were obtained politically, through violent resistance.

Naturally, Jesus' words on that mountaintop directly challenged the present-day ideologies of peace. If there were any questions about what this looked like, one only needed to visit the Gethsemane scene where Jesus rebuked Peter for defending him with a sword. Not only did Jesus' peace practices confront the thinking of his people, they also exposed the brute peace of the Pax Romana as empty propaganda. Lest we count ourselves out, Jesus' peace talk is just as controversial today as it was then. And every bit as relevant.

When we read the seventh oracle, we are reminded that happiness cannot be taken hostage by our enemies or by our powerlessness; but it is taken hostage by our unwillingness to make peace. That's not to say that peacemaking is easy. In fact, it's not. But if we have come this far on the happy trail, we know that Jesus's happy oracles are not merely a bunch of smiley-faced stickers being passed out to the world. He's strategically forging a divine courage made up of the mettle of meekness, mercy, and pure heartedness, and when these strengths come together, they are bravely set for peacemaking.

As we walk through Jesus' happy attitudes, there is a real temptation to search out the exceptions to the rule. Then we make the exceptions the rule and the rule the exception. We may be tempted to raise endless hypotheticals as though we are trying to avoid Jesus' judgment on us. Jesus is not casting judgment on anyone. He is saying his people—the salt, light and City on a Hill—are peacemakers and they are really happy. His people aren't yelling from their soapboxes, scheming from behind closed doors, or ignoring the problem. Instead, they are actively listening from their hearts, learning from their enemies, and making peace happen. My people understand that happiness is not determined by *where* we live but by *how* we live. Happiness is not determined by *what they do,* but by *who we are.* Jeremiah and Jesus go as far as to say that making peace with your enemy is the most responsible thing you can do to find happiness.

Peacekeepers or Peacemakers

For the sake of distinction, notice for a moment that Jesus didn't guide his audience into being peace-*keepers* but peace-*makers*. What follows is not meant to speak disparagingly of peacekeepers. Peacekeeping has its place and does its brand of good in the world. We simply point out that Jesus' vision is more active and seeks to make peace where there is none, and not only keep peace where it already exists.

Peacekeepers	**Peacemakers**
Seeks to keep the peace from a position of power, threat, intimidation, and authority. E.g., police officers, occupational forces, and U. N. peacekeeping troops.	Seeks to make peace from a position of weakness, vulnerability, and powerlessness. E.g., Jesus, Nelson Mandela, Gandhi, Leymah Gbowee
Seeks the absence of conflict, strife, and war.	Seeks whole reconciliation; harmony in relationships and equality. E.g., First century church of Antioch (Acts 11), Christian Peacemaker Teams.
Keeps peace through conflict resolution and anger management, not through inner work. E.g., Occupational Forces, NATO Peacekeeping forces.	Make peace by laying their life down; sacrificing themselves. They make peace through deep inner work. E.g., Jesus, Martin Luther King, Jr.
Seeks peace as a means to stabilize the present systems of power and control.	Seeks peace for the good and benefit of all parties.
Seeks control and conformity.	Seeks freedom and responsibility.
Within a household, wants to avoid conflict.	Within a household, seeks to understand each other, thrive and be happy.

Within a workplace, avoids confrontation.	Within a workplace, seeks to communicate and understand.
Within a community group, leave just to keep the peace.	Within a community group, practices Matthew 18 in resolving conflict
Enforces peace through threat of violence.	Empowers peace through non-violent resistance.

Nelson Mandela's autobiography, *Long Walk to Freedom* , puts into perspective the kind of freedom that peacemaking really achieves for everyone, oppressor and oppressed:

> It was during those [twenty-seven years of imprisonment] that my hunger for the freedom of my own people became a hunger for the freedom of all people, white and black. I knew as well as I knew anything that the oppressor must be liberated just as surely as the oppressed. A man who takes away another man's freedom is a prisoner of hatred. He is locked behind the bars of prejudice and narrowmindedness. I am not truly free if I am taking away someone else's freedom, just as surely as I am not free when my freedom is taken from me. The oppressed and the oppressor alike are robbed of their humanity. When I walked out of prison, that was my mission, to liberate the oppressed and the oppressor both.[75]

We all have encountered those who are disturbers of peace, keepers of peace, and makers of peace. Being a keeper is much better than being a disturber and can be a valiant place to start. For Jesus, though, there is a happiness in actively, assertively, and intentionally making peace. This happy call is for wherever peace is absent—work, home, friendships, neighbors, country, online community—the peacemaker makes peace everywhere. Since this is easier said than done, let's look next at how it's done.

Pax Christi

Humanity is notorious for drawing lines in the sand and building walls on the earth. We scrawl out a hostile line between us and God, and then construct walls between us and "those people." These default behaviors are another consequence from Eden's tree of the knowledge of good and evil. We are intoxicated with this knowledge and can't help but label each person we meet as an "us" (good) or "them" (evil). The toxins from this fruit subconsciously activated emotes a distrust and disdain in all our relationships.

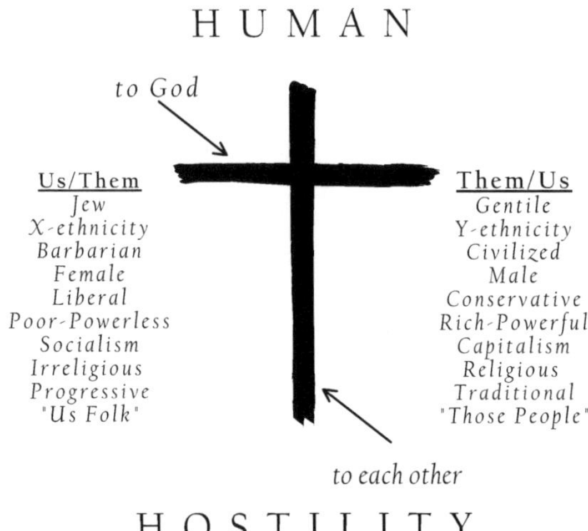

Paul singles out the human condition as one of hostility: hostility between us and God (Eph. 2:14-16) that manifests between "Jew or Greek, slave or free, male or female" (Gal. 3:28).

Peacemaker, used only one time in the entire Bible, appears to be coined here by Jesus. There was one daily activity that put this peacemaking initiative into practice for Jesus—a shared table, also known as commensality. Recent scholarship has unearthed the centrality of the table in the world of Jesus. Because the priests regulated the Temple and elders governed the local synagogue, the table was all that was left. So, Jesus fixed his peace-mission flag smack dab in the middle of the table. He heretically crossed religious, political and social lines when he ate with sinners, publicans, and sex workers. His peace meals with the tax-collectors Zacchaeus and Matthew almost caused a revolt. Allowing an unnamed sex worker to hang out with him at Simon the Pharisee's house brought about harsh criticism. In one controversial scene after another in Luke, Jesus prepares a table in the presence of his enemies. He enacts his final peacemaking covenant around a table with bread and wine, body and blood. In a final poetic peacemaking attempt he reaches over the table to Judas, offering even his betrayer bread and wine. The many peacemaking attempts around the table have led a chorus of scholars to claim Jesus was executed for blurring the social lines around a table.

The table, however, was not the only symbolic place of peacemaking. What began at a table, culminated in a cross, the ultimate peacemaking symbol.

Paul explains to those encountering this peace, that it came at the price of great sacrifice. Paul's motif of costly peace comes up in every letter he writes. To the Corinthians, Paul reminds them of the sacrifice of the "Lord's death" and how Christ's table offers an end to discrimination.[76] Most pointedly, in a letter to Colossae, he draws a thick horizontal line of demarcation with God on one side and us on the other and calls this hostility "alienation, enmity, and estrangement." Then, he drafts a vertical line through the horizontal one and calls it God's "peacemaking through the bloodstained cross." (Colossians 1:20, PT)

"and through him to reconcile to himself all things, whether on earth or in heaven, making peace by the blood of his cross." Colossians 1:20

Peacemaking, therefore, as God enacts it, involves God who *is* an infinite giving away of love, mercy and goodness, and us who are distrustful, fearful and obsessed with death. We have drawn a line in the sand making God our rival and Death our ruler. By death, we built cities, claimed nations, covered up jealousies, destroyed enemies, and solved our problems. We live and die by death. And those we don't trust must die or be scape-goated to a figurative death.

God *crossed* our line in the sands-of-time through Jesus. Through a vulnerable womb, in an off-the-beaten-path village, he offered a vertical response to our horizontal line, a harmless dove of peace descending from the heartrending skies. He was a simple homeless preacher without any political connections, military backing, or academic credentials. He didn't take back the Temple or commandeer synagogues, but unthreateningly made fishing boats into platforms and common everyday tables into podiums. *The medium was the message.*

We responded to this message in predictable fashion. Death. Death is always our answer. And the death we chose in apropos was a cross. God knew our condition, knew we would react this way, and still chose peace over "making an example out of us."

Then we buried it, covered it up as if no one would know. But God fulfilled his peace mission and raised up the innocent Jesus. This time showing us that Death could be defeated by love. His sacrifice became a mirror for anyone willing to look. And for those who look and believe this sacrificial peace offering, death is finally overthrown. In Jesus' sacrifice, we finally see how God is utterly peaceful toward us. The effect of this sacrifice brings together Jews and Gentiles, heaven and earth, justice and mercy, merging all our antonyms with all our synonyms.

Peacemaking not only means something gets sacrificed, but that something gets resurrected.

Carl Jung saw the cross as a universal archetype that represents the unity of opposites, the peacemaking of oppositions. The convergence of the vertical with the horizontal is the symbolic place where thesis and antithesis finally resolve in synthesis.

Jesus' cross did just this! It brought together four Roman soldiers and four Jewish women. It brought together all the competing languages of his world—Aramaic, Greek and Latin—in one message. It hung together the innocent with the condemned. It brought together heaven and earth, God and man. And in that convergence of opposites, a Roman centurion made peace with God, a condemned criminal made peace with death, and now Paul says people as far away as Colossae can make peace with each other. The cross reminds us that peace is found in the intersection and resolution of opposites.

What Paul does at the end of this letter is a brilliant subversion of the Pax Romana: "Let the peace of Christ rule your hearts." The cross of the Pax Romana demanded peace or be killed. In contrast, the cross of the Pax Christi was the self-sacrifice of Christ for the peace of the world. The scandalous symbol Rome used to enforce peace, Christ subverts and uses to empower peace.

The message to us: let the Christ-like peace govern your heart—and once again, we see the happiness that Jesus offers comes back to the heart.

"X" Marks the Spot

For Betty Williams, an Irish Protestant, and Mairead McGuire, a staunch Irish Catholic, the intersection of heaven and earth was found on a street corner where three children lay dead, the collateral damage of the Northern Ireland Conflict. These two moms, from opposite sides of the war, linked arms, bridged the gap and formed The Community for Peace People. Arm in arm, they helped bring down the decades' long violence in Northern Ireland. For Jody Williams, a Vermont Catholic girl, peace-making came in the form of a leaflet on landmines that showed how every twenty minutes a landmine claimed another victim around the world. Jody bridged the gap between opposing militaries and the innocent bystanders.

The point at which oppositional views, attitudes, values, worlds, and understandings intersect is the place where we begin the peacemaking. The world's polarities, whether it's liberal versus conservative, religious versus irreligious, traditional versus progressive, are incredible opportunities for the happy army to break down barriers, build bridges, find common ground, and extend the olive branch.

This image of a cross helps us understand what we undertake when we go about peacemaking. Even at the most elementary level, we are bringing together opposite opinions. At the start of our happy journey, we suggested the oracles were intentionally sequential. Now we can clearly see how meekness, mercy, and pure-heartedness are prerequisites to brokering peace in our world.

Making Means Doing

"We do not think ourselves into new ways of living, we live ourselves into new ways of thinking."[77] We come to this point of the book, so much information, so much knowledge, and if we are not careful, we can assume that with just a little bit more information we will be transformed, and everything will be better. Humans tend to think that knowledge somehow equates to happiness. Jesus knew this human tendency and, as he was wrapping up his thoughts on the happy life, he said, "If you just use my words in Bible studies and don't work them into your life, you are like a stupid carpenter who built his house on the sandy beach... it collapsed like a house of cards." (Matthew 7:26-27, MSG)

Jesus was saying our lives are doomed to a sad fate if we don't put His words into action. Jesus is clear on this point: at the consummation of faith and action transformation takes place. He didn't say, "Take up my words and form discussion groups." That's what philosophers do. He didn't say "Take my teachings and form classrooms." That's what teachers do. He said, "Take up your cross and follow me." He said *move* with me. That's something only God can say. Act. Move. Do. Step out. Go. Move *with me,* means "I'm on the move, you're with me."

So how do we start with peace-making?

Six Smooth Stones that Build a Peace Altar

In practical terms, we want to give you six stones that build altars of peacemaking in your home, neighborhood, community, or work. As we build this six-stoned altar of peace, we want to remind you that peacemaking is a self-sacrificing work. We are not making the sacrifice Jesus did, but we will follow in his footsteps and make sacrifices for peace in our daily lives and for some of us, they will be bigger than others. Peace can cost us something as small as our pride, or an evening of hosting a meal, or something as great as our lives. That is between us and God. What we know is there is a special happiness for building this altar.

First, *prayer is the most significant work of peacemakers.* The moment we bend a knee and ask for peace, we lay the first peace stone. Leymah Gbowee was a devout Liberian Christian. In 2001, she received the Nobel Peace Prize for bringing the Liberian Civil War to a close. Gbowee said she did everything through prayer. She prayed before every meeting, prayed at the meetings, prayed after the meetings. She prayed without ceasing for peace. She said peace never would have come to Liberia without prayer. Prayer fuels us for the peacemaking journey, clarifies the issues, gives us a starting point and, most importantly, removes our isolationism and connects us with the God of Peace.

Second, *peace is a choice.* We place our second stone on the altar when we choose to be peacemakers. Jeremiah knew the exiles had a choice when they arrived in Babylon, they would either choose to sulk in unhappiness or choose shalom. If they chose to make others happy, they would have happiness too. All of the captives had witnessed the killing of friends and family, choosing to not fight and retaliate seemed unjust and even immoral; and yet, seeking peace was God's way, the best way to a happy life. We see captives like Daniel make this choice and because of this choice, Israel prospered and were returned back home.

Third, *peacemaking is an act of bringing together the disparate parties.* After graduating Eastern Mennonite University and during the Liberian Civil War, Leymah Gbowee had a dream where she brought together Muslim women and Christian women to pray, to seek peace and to lead the charge on peace in their war-ravaged country. She acted on this not knowing how it would turn out, but trusting God in prayer to guide the process. She believed if she got the women together, peace would come. The conflict in Ireland followed a similar pattern, getting the moms from both factions together. Getting them together to pray, to express their pain in art—song, painting, and poetry.

Fourth, *listening is where the trust and compassion comes from for peace.* The first and greatest commandment: "Hear, O Israel . . ." states that love is preceded by listening. This principle is universal. There is not peace without first giving someone their voice. When we sit down and hear our enemy's story, understand the fear, the loss, the pain that they have experienced moves on our hearts. Desmond Tutu, who oversaw the Truth and Reconciliation Tribunals in South Africa, mapped out a Fourfold Path to Forgiveness.[78] The first path, he said, is "telling the story." In many of the meetings, this step alone brought peace. Something as simple as saying, "I want to hear your story, your experience" can lead to understanding, understanding then leads to wisdom, and wisdom leads to love.

Fifth, *after listening, pause to acknowledge their pain and give witness to their truth. This starts the healing.* Maya Angelou said, "There is no greater agony than bearing an untold story inside of you." Much work has been done recently by psychologists in studies on "bearing witness." This therapeutic model's premise is that much healing and peace comes from the recovery of voice in the presence of a witness. The healing of the divine-human rift comes down to Jesus sending out his disciples to "be witnesses" to his life, death, and resurrection. The empowerment and healing, the peace and rest that comes from the other giving verbal witness to the story, pain, loss, and grief cannot be overstated.

Sixth, the work of peacemaking is a work of empowering forgiveness. Jesus appears to the dispirited disciples where they are fearfully huddled together. From his essence, he breathes into them peace ("Peace be unto you") and then commissions them as Agents of Peace. He then says, "If you forgive anyone's sins, their sins are forgiven; if you do not forgive them, they are not forgiven."[79] Jesus goes as far to say that the responsibility that comes with housing the Holy Spirit is offering forgiveness to the world. This is squarely on our shoulders. The world bears hostility when we neglect the empowering work of forgiveness that the Holy Spirit has breathed into us.[80]

The cross we are carrying is the intersection of opposites. Peacemakers bear crosses and, with these crosses, build Happy Bridges. Transformation from a drab and listless existence into a happy and rewarding existence happens when we just get out and start living this stuff. That is where God is, and that is where he meets us. Unhappiness, by contrast, is the result of inaction and indifference. Peacemaking will look different for all of us, but as we follow in The Way, we will be led into it, we will recognize our crosses and we will be ready to bear them and experience surprising joy in so doing.

Shalom

Shalom was the feeling of comradery and solidarity that the Head Leader of Kurds had as Mike fastened the Center for National Renewal pin on his lapel. The Kurdish peacemaker felt noticed, affirmed, and championed. Mike shared in both the creation of that moment and the experience of the happy emotion. Shalom-happiness is the feeling of social harmony and emotional balance. All the feelings of goodness accompany the spreading of shalom. In these moments we sense the joy of being children of God and being a force for good in the world. The feeling flows through our spiritual center and out to our emotional makeup and then into our social world leaving us with a sense of wholeness. As we happy makers share the heavenly shalom, a residue of its reverential joy abides in our heart.

❖ My Happy Declaration

I am prepared by meekness, mercy and pure-heartedness to begin my assignment as a Peacemaker. I understand the difference between peacekeeping and peacemaking. The way I will make peace is by accepting my cross of sacrifice for the peace of others. Like Jesus was given the title Son of God at his baptism, I will be rewarded the title, Child of God, when I make peace, and like Jesus, I will be filled with great joy.

➢ Up Next: Happy are the persecuted...(Matt 5:10)

Finally, it is time to blaze our trail into the toughest happy topic of all... suffering. Or more poignantly, persecution. By now you've experienced the gradations of Jesus' happy path and how one inner transformation prepares us for deeper, more profound joy. In the next chapter, our trail finally summits to the peak of happiness.

CHAPTER 11

THE MERRY MARTYR

Finding A Joy Worth Dying For

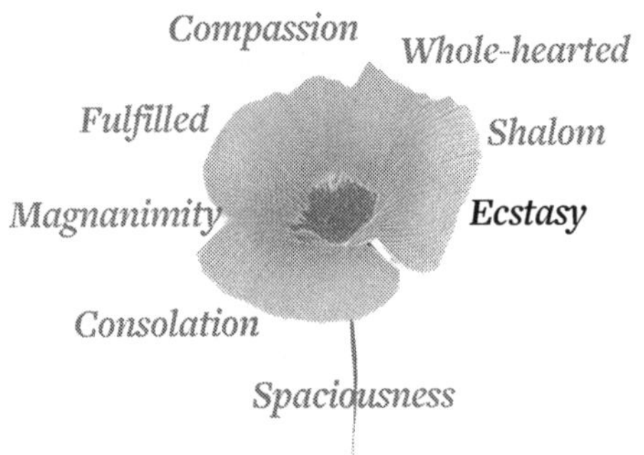

> *Jesus promised his disciples three things - that they would be completely fearless, absurdly happy and in constant trouble.*
>
> —G.K. Chesterton

Mike: In 1968, the U.S. was at the height of the Vietnam conflict. I had just graduated high school and found myself classified 1a. That meant that I could be drafted into the Armed Forces any day. A lot of my friends had been drafted and were serving in the army in Vietnam. I had mixed emotions about it. Sometimes I wanted to be there with them, and sometimes I was glad that I was home. But the memories from that war as a young man put a strange longing in my soul that someday I wanted to go there. In January 2013, I finally made that trip. I was invited by Vietnamese church leaders to come and train pastors.

I didn't really know what to expect. The leaders invited me to a luncheon to meet twelve of the top pastors from the country who oversaw hundreds of churches. The food they had prepared was delicious, and when the lunch was finished, it was time for me to speak to the group at the table.

"Before I speak, I would enjoy hearing your stories."

I asked them to go one by one around the table.

By the time they finished, I could hardly speak. I gently wept listening to their stories. Among the twelve men who shared their experience with Christ and their calling into ministry, I added up more than fifty years spent in Vietnamese prisons for preaching the gospel. One white-haired gentleman was in his 80s and had just finished eight years in a prison.

Their stories moved me, but their demeanor shocked me. The memory of that moment will live with me forever.

The joyful laughter filled the room as these men used humor to share about the persecution they endured for preaching the Gospel. Karl Barth said, "Laughter is the closest thing to the grace of God" and at lunch that day I experienced the grace of God in their blissful suffering.

One of the men said to his friend, "You preached John 3:16 to me then said, 'Now you go and do the same as I did here today for you.' I had preached only two days when I was arrested and put in prison. I spent nine months in solitary confinement, but God told me I'd be in here nine months like a baby is in the womb and when I come out, I'm going to do miraculous things. I spent nine months in solitary, and when I was released, God worked miraculous things like He promised. The son of a top communist leader was in prison with me for drugs and my testimony to him led him to an experience with Jesus. He was set free from an addiction to heroin. His father was so thankful, that when I was released, he met with me and said," You preach anywhere you want to, anytime, and if you get arrested, you just have them call me and I'll get you out of trouble!"

The joy that these men expressed between themselves, let me know that the promise Jesus made had been fulfilled in their lives. Their persecution and imprisonment and beatings had resulted in a beautiful Heavenly fraternity. A happy brotherhood of the greatly rewarded. Their joy was greater than I had ever seen. I was so moved that I will never forget them. I made a covenant that day with those precious men to pray for them and support their work and to remember them. I still do to this day.

Our media-driven world inundates us with images of happiness—the peaceful retiree on a dream vacation, smiling spouses enjoying a fine dining experience, the adventurer skydiving, and the van life enthusiast. The message: pleasure is happiness, and happiness means being in total control. Being our own boss, managing our family, mapping our future, and completing our five and ten-year goals with only mild adjustments defines the happy life. We see the loss of control as the beginning of suffering and a combatant to our happiness. Maintaining happiness means we work to eliminate pain, avoid suffering, and maintain control.

And yet, much of life is outside our control. The flat tire. The missing parts of the online purchase. The stock markets. The economy. The election. The earthquake. The pandemic. The cancer. The terminal illness. The premature death.

And part of life is under the control of others. Our boss. Our teacher. Our spouse. Our parent. Our child. The governor. The President.

What does this mean for our happiness when so much of life is outside of our control?

Boethius, the beloved sixth century Christian philosopher, wrestled with this very question. He was falsely accused of treason, imprisoned and tortured, while his wife and two children were reduced to poverty. He watched the king's court take away everything that had brought him so much joy. His body, routine, estate, future, and even his life was controlled by the state. He lamented, "I am banished from all happiness."[81] His persecution ultimately was the loss of control and freedom.

From his prison cell Boethius writes one of the most moving works on happiness.

Lady Wisdom appears to him in several visions and philosophizes about real happiness in the face of his existential questions. We can relate to his questions and longing for substantive answers. With so much of life outside of our control, does it mean that happiness is also outside our control? What, if anything, can be done to be happy when we suffer? Is our happiness dependent on good fortune that happens to us, good things that go our way? Or is happiness an undisturbed good thing within us, even when bad comes our way?

Those questions seem even more relevant today. Recently, people from around the globe were invited to send in questions they had about happiness and get answers from a Christian Bishop and a Buddhist monk. "The most asked question was not about how we could discover our own joy but how we could possibly live with joy in a world filled with so much suffering."[82]

For those of us who come to this final Beatitude for an answer to these questions, we find Jesus' last oracle to be prophetically timeless and, if we are honest, downright absurd, especially given the fact that he offers no disclaimers.

> *Happy are the persecuted for theirs is the kingdom of heaven.*
>
> —Jesus' eighth word on happiness.

The seven happy oracles, not unlike a pilgrimage, lead us through different landscapes each with their own happy view. But when we finally arrive at Death Valley, this barren wasteland of suffering, we are stumped. And it's here that we are tempted to reassess our choice of happy. Here in this insufferable setting, surely "blessed" makes more sense. Who in their right mind would or could be happy in suffering? Maybe the world's happy propaganda was right all along.

However, recent scholarship on the history of happiness stands pat. Any reader of the first century would have associated *makarios* (Matthew's word for happy), with the tradition of Greek philosophy on happiness. One happiness historian goes as far as to say that what Jesus does here, especially in this eighth happy oracle, is offer a shockingly new happiness.[83] Happiness was a highly philosophized topic by Socrates, Plato, Aristotle, and Seneca the Younger in the five centuries leading up to that Spring hillside lecture with Rabbi Jesus. Greek philosophy emphasized the good life, Latin philosophers emphasized the bucolic life, and Hebrew teachers emphasized the life of wisdom. And, although Jesus' happy oracles have trailed through Prophetic meadows, Wise plains, and Torah valleys in the previous seven happy statements, we now cross the border into new authorial territory.

In fact, the ground is so new that Jesus will use a literary convention of his day, Hebrew Parallelism, repeating the same concept in slightly different and nuanced ways to reinforce what he's saying, just in case we think we misheard him.

- Happy are those who are persecuted ... for theirs is the kingdom of heaven.
- Happy are you when others...persecute you...for your reward is great in heaven.

There are several reasons for this parallelism:

1. This point is not to be missed.
2. This is the cumulative and climactic point of the previous seven.
3. He doesn't want them to mistake suffering as some kind of curse to happiness.
4. The outcome of this happy attitude is doubly happy.

Although many Westerners, especially United States citizens, have never faced the kind of persecution Jesus speaks of, it's important to pause for perspective. The U.S. Christian is a tiny fraction of faithful Jesus followers who are well represented globally and historically. The numbers of people who suffer around the globe for doing right and for following their faith is astonishing, but it's nothing new; it's always been this way. In light of that, Jesus' words are incredibly relevant, and as we shall see, have happy meaning also to those free from persecution.

The words Jesus uses as his descriptors of the happy life—persecute, insult and false-witness—are straightforward words and come from the Greek and Hebrew meaning "to chase." To be persecuted is to be preyed upon.

It's absolutely mindboggling how so many in church history missed this very point. Jesus did not say, "Blessed are those who persecute the heretics, infidels, and unbelievers." He did not say, "It's more blessed to persecute than be persecuted!" Or, "Blessed are you when you criticize, judge, and shame the evil doers." His vision is that our good works would subvert Satan's evil empire.

The practice of the better is the best criticism of the bad.[84] Jesus is saying the practice of his happy way is the best criticism of the world's happiness. And when that practice is practiced well, it frequently results in persecution. And that is okay. Our practice of Jesus' new happiness is the best possible critique of the world's pseudo-happiness.

Two Kinds of Persecution

A brief word here on suffering and persecution. The eighth happy oracle is not addressing suffering in general, but a specific kind of suffering—persecution. That is not to say that Jesus doesn't bless other kinds of suffering, he does. But Jesus knows that his own practice of these happy oracles will result in persecution for himself and many of his followers, so he doubly affirms that not even persecution can jeopardize real joy.

Jesus in other settings speaks about general human suffering due to natural disasters or physical ailments. He moves with compassion for our suffering, much of which is unjust and some of which is justifiable. In both cases, he feels compassion and suffers with us. The thief suffering alongside of him on the cross receives forgiveness. The woman caught in the act of adultery is rescued from a lynch-mob. Those suffering from visual and mental impairments are healed. Although this happy oracle isn't about these kinds of suffering, he affirms in the returning prodigal, the rejoicing Samaritan woman, and the healed Bartimaeus that all suffering can lead to joy. The point being, no matter the source of our suffering, happiness and suffering can be inextricably linked.

Now that we've established the difference, let's return our focus on happiness and persecution. In this double oracle, Jesus differentiates persecution *for righteousness' sake* (verse ten) from persecution *for Jesus' name's sake* (v.11), claiming both are happily blessed. For our purposes, we clarify the "persecution for righteousness' sake" as the persecution that arises when we set about to make the world just and right. We define persecution for Jesus' name's sake as the persecution that comes about for those who are persecuted for their religious beliefs.

Dietrich Bonhoeffer, German theologian, who was hanged for his resistance of Hitler, wrote about the beatitudes in his book, *The Cost of Discipleship*, where he said of verse ten, "This does not refer to the righteousness of God, but to suffering in a just cause."[85] In other words, Jesus does not say, "blessed are the orthodox believers who suffer for righteousness." Neither does he qualify the kind of righteousness as though there is some doctrinal prerequisite. Yes, he is speaking to Jews, but he is speaking about justice, any and all kinds of justice, wherever it is found, whoever is persecuted for it. He is saying that those who suffer for justice are happily bringing heaven to earth.

Persecution for Righteousness. Persecution for justice often, though not always, shows up as wrongful imprisonment. In our research of the Innocence Project and Innocence Network, we found a mysterious outcome associated with wrongful imprisonments. Story after story told of people wrongly prosecuted and imprisoned that come out on the other side kinder, compassionate, humble, and even forgiving. Anthony Hinton spent twenty-eight years on death row in a wrongful incarceration. After the Supreme Court overturned his case, he wrote a book called, *The Sun Does Shine: how I found life and freedom on death row.* As absurd as it sounds, he claims that what he suffered in prison is responsible for his bright spirit, good life, and a just cause to which he has dedicated his life.

Numerous books and talks have been given by survivors of the Jewish Holocaust, South African apartheid, and other ethnic cleansings from around the globe whose words of forgiveness and gratitude are little human miracles.

Those who do justice love people. And frequently, this love for the marginalized, outcast, and minority brings the righteous doer under persecution. Jorge Valls spent twenty years of torture in Fidel Castro's jails for his humanitarian activism. He said, "I have never in my entire life been as free as when I was in prison. Why? Because defeated, humiliated, famished. . there was one thing that remained deep within me: my dignity, my interior freedom. This is what made me forgive my persecutors. Forgiveness puts us above woe, hate, disdain. My enemy became my brother." When you read Valls account, you get the sense that there is a deep river of happiness, an undefeatable joy that is possible.

Nelson Mandela spent twenty-seven years in prison for his fight against apartheid. His case is interesting because he sets out as an angry activist, but after twenty-seven years of imprisonment he is filled with compassion, even for his enemies. Through the suffering, he came to see them as his brothers, molded by the same societal fears that shaped him. Look at a picture of him from before and then after prison. The hardness is replaced with a peaceful joy.[86]

Sophie Scholl, a nineteen-year old student at the University of Munich, was seized for spreading anti-Nazi leaflets and refused to recant, so they led her away to be executed. Prison guards described her brave composure as she stepped forward and said, "How can we expect righteousness to prevail when there is hardly anyone willing to give himself up individually to a righteous cause? Such a fine, sunny day, and I have to go, but what does my death matter, if through us, thousands of people are awakened and stirred to action?"

That single act of publishing leaflets was hungering and thirsting for justice. And that thirst got her beheaded. According to Jesus, it is not just the work of justice that is kingdomly, *but it's also the very act of being persecuted* for the act of justice. That Sophie Scholl valued God's justice above her own life gives witness to the existence of an otherworldly kingdom, one that she saw even though others were blind. She died as though a life cut short in doing right was worth more than sixty more years of time on earth. In other words, *the nobility and joy of dying for what was right, far exceeded all the pleasures and experiences of sixty more years of life.*

Below is a list of people who were persecuted for righteousness:

- The Ten Boom Family incarcerated in concentration camps for harboring Jews.
- William Lloyd Garrison dragged through the streets and almost lynched for his antislavery speech.
- Maximilian Kolbe, Franciscan friar, volunteered to take the place of a Jewish father and be starved to death in a Nazi concentration camp.
- Rosa Parks arrested for refusing to move to the back of the bus.

- Malala Yousafzai shot by the Taliban for advocating for girls' education.
- Aung San Suu Kyi arrested for fifteen years for her advocacy of a free Burma.

Persecuted for Loving God. In the second persecuted statement, Jesus adjusts the meaning a little. He personalizes it from "Happy are the persecuted for justice's sake" to "Happy are you when . . .persecuted for my sake." The shift brings a focus to those who are persecuted in their love for God. From the primitive stoning of the first martyr Stephen to graphic social media produced beheadings by the Islamic State militants, many have suffered persecution for their love of Jesus. Persecution in other countries takes on the form of imprisonment, public shaming, economic sanctions, and exile status.

Each generation, from Christ's time to the present, and each family of origin, from Adam to the United Nations, have not been without an authentic witness to the realness of Jesus' kingdom. Whether persecuted or martyred, our world has been left with witness after witness that the real happy life cannot be tortured away, burned away, persecuted away, or even discomfited away. What Jesus offers, and the persecuted can attest to, walks unthwarted through tribulation, trial, and distress, coming out evermore happy and joyful.

Jesus' point and the testimony of two thousand years is that no matter how you suffer, why you suffer, or what you suffer, joy cannot be robbed from you. They can take your possessions, inflict you with pain, destroy your reputation, but no one can take your joy! Why can't joy be taken? For Jesus this is true because joy is God and God is joy, and these realities are so deep within that they are beyond the reach of Nazi Guards, Roman Gladiators, and Dictator's power. When we suffer this deeply, we finally get in touch with the deepest part of our spirit, that estuary where the Ocean of God mingles with the rivers of man. The experience as reported by so many can be cleansing, healing, freeing, empowering and revelatory. How can this be so?

God is Suffering

The late René Girard, world renowned philosopher and literary critic, came to a deep trust in God much later in life through the study of literature. He points out that in antiquity the gods are with the successful, powerful, the *majority scrutiny*, the kings who conquer and the nations who conquest. This is necessary to legitimize the gods. However, in the Hebrew Bible, Girard read of a God said to be with the oppressed, the suffering, and the marginalized. Hebrew stories say God was with the stand-alone Noah building an ark, the radical Abraham leaving Ur and the betrayed and enslaved Joseph. God was with David, an unwanted shepherd boy, with the crying fugitive Hagar, and the oppressed Hannah, and God made covenant with Israel, a tiny nation of slaves.

When the Christians turn the page, we discover that this God who has always been with the victim has now *become* the victim. It's no wonder atop this mountain Jesus makes suffering his doubly happy word. Then, when he is glorified on the Mount of Transfiguration with Moses and Elijah, he talks again, "about his death that would happen in Jerusalem" (Luke 9:31). When he is in his most ecstatic state, he's talking about suffering! And Hebrews says, "who for the joy that was set before him endured the cross" (Heb 12:2, KJV).

Jesus modeled to his earliest followers that suffering is not something to be avoided, coped with, or endured, but a means by which we were present with God.

Socrates dies stoically, Samson heroically, Cato via harikari, Judah Maccabee valiantly. But it's Jesus who does all the above *and* joyfully. It's Jesus who sees the cross as enthronement, the crucifixion as his finest hour, and from that elevated *stauros,* his joyous glory is revealed to all creation.

Suffering with those Who Suffer

By being the God who in Hebrew scripture was with the suffering and in Christian scripture became the suffering, we are given a model of how to enter into the joy of suffering, even when we are not the one being persecuted.

Chiune Sugihara, a compassionate Christian and a high-ranking Japanese diplomat was demoted in 1939 for refusing to support Japan's war machine. He was sent off to be a one man consulate in Kovno, Lithuania.

When he arrived, Jewish refugees from Poland and other Nazi occupied territories were flooding into Lithuania. In defiance of the Japanese government and before they could recall him, he wrote a total of 6,000 transit visas for Jews fleeing Hitler. Sugihara was unceremoniously dismissed from his diplomatic status, dishonored in his country, and forced to work in Russia to support his family.

In 1968, a Sugihara survivor located him and thanked him, after which thousands came forward to honor him. Today there are well over 100,000 descendants alive because of the Sugihara family. In 1985, a year before he died, he received Israel's highest honor, as he was recognized as Righteous Among the Nations.

Although Sugihara wasn't being persecuted, he chose to suffer alongside the Jewish people.

Most of us reading this book live with freedom of religion, speech, and even the right to pursue happiness. We may wonder how this happy oracle that meant so much to Jesus and his first followers can mean anything to us. Jesus boldly declares that when you suffer with those who suffer through support, care, and mercy works, your joyful reward is equivalent to those who suffer.

Sugihara's life illustrates this very point. For almost thirty years he was relegated to obscurity and a substandard life. Then a little over a decade before he died, one person showed up to say thank you and then another and another. This kind of happiness is far richer, deeper and wider than the highest rank he could have achieved.

Speaking at the National Prayer Breakfast, U2 musician Bono described how God is with us when we suffer with the suffering ones:

> "God is in the slums, in the cardboard boxes where the poor play house. God is in the silence of a mother who has infected her child with a virus that will end both their lives. God is in the cries heard under the rubble of war. God is in the debris of wasted opportunity and lives, and God is with us if we are with them."

To this end, Jesus does not see suffering as the enemy of happiness—something to be overcome, avoided or resisted. In the Fourth Gospel, what the disciples see as the gruesome persecution of the cross, Jesus calls the hour of his greatest glory. In fact, he goes so far as to theologize it as his enthronement, the place where he is inaugurated as the cosmic King in Latin, Greek, and Hebrew. The writer of Hebrews connects the cross and joy together. The persecution is the glory of God, and all believers are summonsed into this fellowship of blessing, happiness, reward, and eternal life.

The Absurdity of Happy Suffering

It would be understandable at this point if you are asking, "How can this make for a happy life?" Sugihara's dishonorable discharge to a remote place in Russia, and Sophie Scholl's youthful execution, and Maximilian Kolbe's death by starvation on the surface seem to be anything but happy!

But there are three realities about life and happiness that Jesus assumes, and that we would do well to consider, before jumping to hasty conclusions.

First, *time is not all that there is to life.* Life has soul. Life has character. Life has story. "It's not the years in your life that count. It's the life in your years."[87] Jesus was more in his three years of ministry than we are in a lifetime.

Second, *Death is not the final word on life, nor the dead end of happiness.* Death is the vehicle by which we arrive at uninterrupted, all consuming, eternal happiness. Death carries us straight into eternal bliss, and in this way, it need not be avoided. How could God allow torturous death to be the last word on his prophets, apostles, saints and beloved who suffered persecution? The only logical answer is that death does not have the final say on happiness.

Third, *the autonomous self is not the goal of a happy human experience.* Autonomy is the great misnomer associated with the meaning of freedom and happiness. "Too much self-centered thinking is the source of suffering. A compassionate concern for others' well-being is the source of happiness."[88] We are reminded that a cloud of witnesses watches from beyond death, a cloud we will join one day. A full orbed happiness cannot be fully experienced in an individual experience, but in the community of fellow sufferers. Jesus assumes this when he says, "...for in the same way they persecuted the prophets who were before you" (Matthew 5:12, NIV).

One historian said "The Stoics had suggested that the happy man could be even happy on the rack, happy in spite of the suffering. Christianity took this a step further, proposing that happiness [came through the suffering]."[89] The word that best describes first-hand account witnesses of the persecuted is ecstasy. We realize how absurd this sounds, but look at the following Happy Martyrs:

"like the face of an angel," the description of Stephen's face while he was being stoned.[90]

"I was in the Spirit on the Lord's Day," John's ecstatic proclamation during his exile and banishment.

"Thanks be to God that I am happier here now than I was in the flesh." Perpetua, Felicita and Saturus give us the first, first-person account of a martyr. Perpetua describes the journey to the arena of beasts as "the road to hope."

"It's a lovely day." Sophie Scholl at her hanging.

"For me the beginning of life...," Bonhoeffer's final words before his beheading. One doctor reported, "in the almost fifty years that I worked as a doctor, I have hardly seen a man die so entirely submissive to the will of God."

And like the soaring Negro Spirituals about heaven that walk us through hell, the one constant in all of these experiences is the way that suffering elevates us in worship into ecstatic realms. In these joyful expressions, the worshipping community is the sign of God's Presence on earth.

The Via Dolorosa

During the Byzantine era Christians mapped out a pilgrimage route which retraced the final steps of Jesus as he was led to his execution site, just outside the walls of Jerusalem. They called it The Via Dolorosa, Latin for "the way of suffering." Today the path includes fourteen stations that commemorate events in Jesus' execution parade. We have identified four motifs along the Via Dolorosa, that move the sufferer along into a noble purpose.

First, discover your why. Why are you suffering? Nietzsche said, "he who has a why can bear almost any how." "Whys" connect our suffering with our meaning and when that happens joy comes alive. Often, in the midst of suffering it is enough to believe there is a why, even if we don't know it yet.

Second, know your who. Who are you suffering with, suffering for, and suffering through. The Psalms frequently connect suffering with, for, and through God. When this happens, love erupts and love always gives birth to joy, always.

Third, be present with God. Many of those who have suffered have expressed that during these times they were closest and nearest to the Presence of God. Why this is, we don't know, but that it happens again and again is the testimony of the many persecuted witnesses.

Fourth, find your meaning. This develops from the first one, in that you fully experience the suffering and when you finally come through it, a noble purpose or meaning has emerged. We have listed a few archetypes that can emerge from suffering:

- Wounded Healer: healing people through your woundedness.
- Broken Peacemaker: making peace through your brokenness
- Oppressed Deliverer: delivering people through your oppression
- Suffering Savior: saving others through your suffering
- Sought-out-Seeker: guiding others through your questions, quests and journey
- Generous Steward: giving to others through your loss
- Happy Martyr: bringing joy to others through your suffering

Notice how the experience of suffering incarnates paradoxical realities. We become wounded and yet healers, victimized and yet victorious. We identify with the greater purpose of our victimization and not the lesser meaninglessness of it. Our broken pieces are one part of the wholeness of peace in the world. Suffering gives us a heart for the victims and a courage for a renewed mission.

Rejoice. In the previous seven happy attitudes, Jesus never calls for rejoicing, but here, he bids his happy sojourners to rejoice, that is to outwardly express the inward joy. In Hebrew thought, rejoicing often took on the forms of singing, dancing, or jubilant exultations. Is Jesus challenging us to suffer happily? Or is he showing us that the one last freedom we have, in a moment when all our freedoms have been stripped, is the choice to choose joy?

Victor Frankl talks of a disarming joy in his memoir from Auschwitz. Suffering made sunsets more beautiful, relationships more real, and longings more exquisite and poetic. He observed that each person, even in Jewish concentration camps, had one freedom the Nazis could not take and that was the freedom to choose an attitude. We get to choose to dignify our suffering with joy, nothing can take that from us. This is not a mind-over-matter thing but an awareness of the real possibility for connecting with the Divine joy that is present with us, especially in our most vulnerable moments.

Authors' Note: We recognize that many of us reading the book enjoy the privilege afforded us by living in a developed country. While we may never be faced with the kinds of suffering referenced in this chapter, we may suffer because we go against the status quo, we speak out against injustices or simply because we choose selflessness. We will likely suffer the microaggressions that come from living an authentic Real Happy life, one which embraces God's dream for society. And when we suffer, not with a martyrs' complex, but with a martyr's happiness, we are really living.

Ecstasy

Ecstasy, the apex of all happy emotions, the feeling that we are being transported into an Otherworldly reality. Ecstasy is the sensation of being elevated into Divine summits where we feel the undying goodness in all of life. It's the ineffable experience of the ultimate meaning of life rushing through our spirit, dancing in our body, and enlightening our minds. Not only does ecstasy stand alone as its own emotion, it is also the zenith experience of the other seven happy emotions. The below excerpt gets at what we mean.

Father Jacques Hammel was murdered by two young jihadists while he celebrated the Eucharist at Saint-Étienne-du-Rouvray on July 26, 2016. Grabbing an elderly parishioner, the two jihadists forced him to use his cell phone to record Father Hammel's murder. They then struck the parishioner down as if to kill him next. He said:

> "I was convinced that I was going to die, but I prayed. I contemplated my life, and I was at peace. I have never been so serene. Completely in peace. I had no remorse, only love in me. In fact, it was a moment of great happiness."

It's absurd to think it, but the reality is that happiness is not really real if we can't experience it at the lowest point of life. We discover, what the world would avoid at all costs in its quest for happiness, the lowest of human lows, persecution, is elevated to the highest of human highs: ecstasy. Yes, it's fitting that ecstasy is paired with persecution. As we summit the final beatitude and survey what we have walked through to get here, there is no doubt that nothing can sabotage Jesus' joy—not poverty, mourning, landlessness, hunger, thirst, being wronged, or being in a wrong world—nothing. In fact, quite the contrary. The experiences and realities the world teaches us to avoid in our quest for happiness become the pathways of Jesus' happy trail. The contrast of ecstasy in moments of inhumane suffering means that God is giving us real joy. That is good news, that is real happiness.

❖ My Happy Declaration

I will overcome my fear and resistance to suffering, understanding that I will be joining a fraternity of the greatest. When I suffer, God has prepared a deep and lasting happiness for me that cannot be taken away, even by death!

➢ Up Next: Happy is he who is not offended in me...(Matt 11:6)

On the heels of the eighth beatitude, it's natural to ask: what about all those who suffered and weren't happy? Sure enough, Jesus never said that everyone who suffered would be happy. He said that persecution is a pathway into happiness. Is there consolation for those who didn't find that path or those who lost their happiness along the way? It so happens that Jesus left a bonus *makarism* for those who lost the trail and want to recover it.

CHAPTER 12

UNOFFENDABLE JOY

Recovering Our Smile

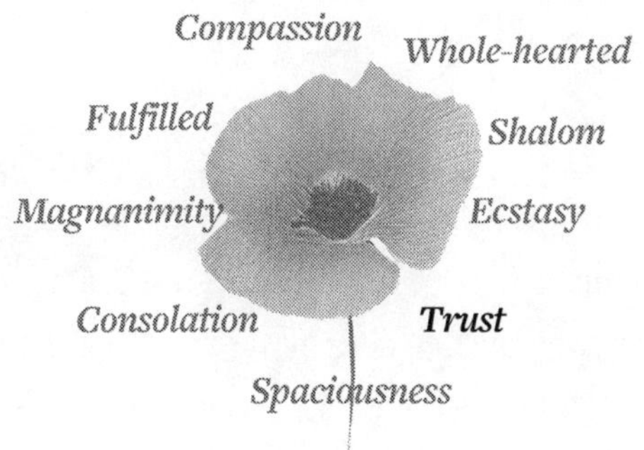

Man is fond of counting his troubles, but he does not count his joys. If he counted them up as he ought to, he would see that every lot has enough happiness provided for it.

—Fyodor Dostoevsky

Mike: We sat scattered on the Galilean hillside. Red poppies like tiny helium balloons floated above the carpet of spring grass. In the not too far distance, the deep blue Galilean Sea shimmered in the late morning sun. I finished reading the last of the beatitudes to our tour group as we reenacted the Sermon on the Mount.

What I said next was unplanned and unscripted but prompted from the Spirit. While I talked with our group from the beatitudes, I felt connected to their life situations. Many of those present had been through significant life hurt in the past year or so. One couple had just buried a family member. A single woman walking through a bitter divorce covered her face with her hands. A dad and mom stood with their arms around each other, praying about a falling out with their daughter. A man in his mid-thirties peered out toward the distant mountain ranges, contemplating how hard he had tried to find his place in life and hadn't landed anywhere. As I looked around, it seemed everyone had experienced disappointments varying in one degree or another.

Feeling a tug from somewhere, I reminded our group that Jesus knew this kind of pain too and had a blessing for those who were doing their best to not get offended. I shared a little bit about what you will read below.

As I talked, one by one, people knelt. A beautiful and holy hush came over us. I cried. They cried. We all sat down on the grass in the solemn reverie. Wordless hope welled up, whispering to us, "all will be ok." On that blanket of red poppies, we all felt like our disappointments and misunderstandings were holy and blessed.

The spirit of that moment stayed with me for the rest of the tour, on the flight home, and for several weeks thereafter. This book has been an attempt at unpacking the sacredness of what happened on that happy poppy day.

Happy Trails

We set out, eight chapters ago, on this happy trail excited, eager and, perhaps, with great expectations. The trailhead advertised, "Happy Kingdom Next Eight Stops." Now, here we are. Congratulations! We've reached the summit! Our view takes in the cotton candy sky, the frosty snow cone mountains, and the winding blueberry rivers. As we survey the miles travelled with Jesus and the terrain lying behind us, we may notice some haven't made the trip.

Along the way, there are many opportunities to second guess the path Jesus offers to the Happy Kingdom. Maybe we overpacked and the weight of attachment was just too much to part with, so we never even got started. Or maybe we took the popular shortcut of self-assertion when Jesus took the longer trek of meekness. Whatever the case, we know along the way there are many detours we can take that veer off Jesus' narrow trail of ascent.

This final chapter, strategically placed in the dust of the Happy Martyr, is for those of us who have suffered and didn't experience the joy that the happy oracles promised. Perhaps we were offended and stumbled in our faith. Yes, there is rich testimony of happiness in suffering. But here is ample evidence of others whose suffering results in disappointment, unfulfilled expectations, and existential futility. People who once had the spark of joy, the beaming smile of gratitude, and a passionate bounce now joylessly sulk and slink and sour.

How do we recover the happiness and joy we once had? How do we shift the backward-facing regrets into forward-facing hope?

Here's the tragedy: joyfulness is not a given. We can lose it somewhere along the way. Jesus knew this. Jesus cared about this, too.

If you have lost the happy trail along the way and want to recover it, this chapter is for you. Jesus' final words are a prophetic promise to those of us who lost our happiness and want to find it again.

Jesus foresaw the long journey and stumbling stones in the path. He understood the temptation to turn back, be offended, get bitter or become jaded. So, he offered a happy oracle to reclaim our path to joy. The previous eight oracles inspired disciples at the beginning of their journey and help us count the cost of the happy life as we trek along. This happy oracle, spoken to a prophet at the end of his journey, helps us catch our second wind and finish the course.

Questions from a Dungeon

Two disciples of John the Baptizer linger, waiting to ask Jesus a question. Their mentor, persecuted for his preaching, now sits on Death Row. Jesus' happy life mantra, smiling novices and Kingdom excitement is not shared by these two Baptizer disciples. They know too much; the rose-colored glasses came off long ago. They wait their turn, with eyes shifting as they assess the Jesus fad that's trending. Everything Jesus taught that day sounded good, but they now know that life isn't that packaged and clean.

The crowd dissipates. Jesus is debriefing with Peter when he notices their nervous glances. He knows who they are and shares their grief and loss. After all, John wasn't just his mentor, he was also family. The baptismal spot where John could always be found washing people into a new way of life was vacant. The loss of John's booming wilderness voice that brought the desert to life was now muffled in the dungeon of a bloodthirsty queen. Their eyes meet. Jesus smiles and waves them over.

"John sent us here to ask you, 'Are you the one-who-is-to-come or shall we look for another?'" (Matthew 11:3)

The question seems out of place. Jesus has just raised a boy from the dead, and it's this news that precedes John's question.

We can't know for sure, but we humbly offer three rationales for John's line of questioning.

First, he is disappointed. Life is not going the way he thought it would. He was doing so much good; his message and movement were in their initial stages of setting up the Messiah. Although his influence had reached the furthest shores of the Greco-Roman world, he had visions of God's Kingdom on Earth. The dungeon chains and rumors of his execution were not how he envisioned his life. Moreover, his younger cousin, Jesus, enjoyed influence and notoriety.

Second, he is impatient. Several scholars point out that the coming of the "Kingdom of God" was taking too long for John. If the Kingdom was here, why was he still in prison? The Kingdom message was "release for prisoners," the year of Jubilee, and the assumed overthrow of Rome! The longer Jesus took to do his "on Earth as it is in Heaven," the less likely he was the one.

Third, Jesus was not fitting John's Messianic expectation. John had a Messiah Checklist, and Jesus was not checking the boxes! (We get more deeply into this one in the following section).

The big three—disappointments, delay, and unfulfilled expectations. In one jail-celled moment, it's easy to imagine, John was experiencing all three. And like for John, any of these can cause us to question our faith and take umbrage at God.

The-One-Who-Is-To-Come

Jesus lived during what historians refer to as the Second Temple Era. The people looked for the "One who was to come," a theological and technical term for the Messiah. There were many different interpretations and opinions as to the "One who was to come."

Pharisees. They believed the "One who is to come" would restore moral order to Israel.

Zealots. For the most part, zealots were a Galilean phenomenon. They believed the "One who was to come" would be a military general or leader overthrowing Rome and establishing a new Davidic reign.

Herodians. King Herod was a client king of the Roman empire. This meant that as long as he had Rome's favor, kept the peace and paid taxes to Rome, he and his family could govern Judea, Samaria, and Idumea. The Herodians included anyone in this region of the Empire who were supporters and benefactors of Herod's political party. Herod considered himself to be the "One who is to come," and sought to bring about the Kingdom Age through city planning, architecture, education, and art.

Sadducees. This political party was comprised of wealthy priestly aristocrats. They interpreted the Scriptures loosely and didn't believe in resurrection, angels, or that there was "One who is to come."

Essenes. This group of apocalyptic Jews is especially relevant to John's disappointment. John was part of their separatist movement.[91] The Essenes thought Herod and the Temple system were a sham. Conspiracy theories abounded related to Rome building Herod's Temple, priests price gouging animals for temple sacrifices, Sadducees and Pharisees having their pockets lined with money from this religious mockery.

The Essenes didn't just look for the "One who is to come" but acted to prepare the way for the Lord. They believed he would arrive once they had completed their work. And when that happened, he would come through the wilderness, march up to Jerusalem and baptize the corrupt systems with fire and judgment. For this reason, they separated from society by living out in the wilderness. Their theme Scripture, "a voice of one crying in the wilderness, prepare the way of the Lord," was John's message and people flocked in anticipation of the "One."

They were moralists, separatists, and pietists who didn't drink fermented drinks, eat meals with impure people, and boycotted the compromised Jerusalem Temple. They fasted three to four days a week to remain pure, and preached harshly against sin and immorality.

The Dove and Voice moment at Jesus' baptism signaled him as The One, but if Jesus was the "One who is to come," why was he violating the purity codes? Turning water to wine? Eating with sinners? Defending his disciples who weren't fasting? Breaking the sabbath code of conduct? We can see how John, as an Essene, would not only question if Jesus was the One, but be disappointed with him, despite his audacious miracles and sanctioned heavenly authority.

How is any of this relevant to us and our quest for happiness?

Whatever we "look for," we expect, and unfulfilled expectations are the source of much of our disappointments.

Moreover, our expectations can blind us to the serendipitous moments erupting outside our line of vision. For John, and for us, our happiness is limited to our expectations. Without realizing it, we put a lid on, a boundary around, and a definition beside our happiness. Then, we timestamp happiness with our own rubbery expiration date. Yes, Jesus just raised a boy from the dead, but if you're expecting Herod to be exposed, judgement to befall Rome, and the Temple to be purified, then a resurrected dead boy doesn't really register on your faith meter. And you won't be happy with anything less.

Conditionally Unoffended

That day in those baptismal waters John beheld his younger cousin and knew this is the "One who is to come." Following heaven's thundering confirmation, Jesus then, like his older cousin, walked out into the wilderness.

We only think of the baptismal moment in terms of Jesus, but have you ever stopped to think what that moment meant to John? In that one moment, the Eternal validated John's baptismal ministry, prophetic message, and wilderness cathedral!

Identifying the One is easy when the heavens boom, the Spirit flutters, the waters flow, and the crowd is wild with awe. Rejoicing in the One is beautiful when he's being baptized in your waters—methods, interpretations, expectations, mission, and values. When you feel his presence and brotherhood is validating your mission, your community, your message and methodology, there is nothing with which to be offended. John can easily trust Jesus; he's family. John can bless his students to study under Jesus since he has baptized him.

Jesus immediately launches his work of Kingdom initiatives. But as time passes, disturbing reports trickle back to John of Jesus' methods. Jesus goes to Jerusalem, participates in Temple worship, sacrifices, and festivals. Jesus cheerfully and liberally forgives sins. The rumor is Jesus is a glutton and boozer. He parties with Rome's henchmen and tax collectors and receives foot massages from prostitutes. He accepts dinner invitations from Pharisees and priests. Jesus seems to be violating every sacred vow of John's ascetic community. The joyous heavenly dove moment is long gone, and John is left with a million questions.

Alas, in this prophet's very human moment, we find someone relatable. We relate with lost joy and clarity. We relate with the incongruence of beautiful starts and not-quite so beautiful developments. We relate with stumbling blocks. We understand how frustrating it is when the One our hearts first recognized, little by little, renders himself unrecognizable. We, too, question and balk when Jesus crosses our theological lines. We relate when it seems the God who is the same yesterday, today and forever, changes.

Salt in the Wound

Reports of Jesus' healing work are what caused John to send the delegation, but then they ask, "should we look for another?" As if to pour salt into the wound, Jesus does not answer John's very direct question. He never says "yes, I am the One."[92] Instead, he says, "Go tell him what you see," turns right back around and keeps healing. Then Jesus gives another *makarism,* a bold clue into recovering and maintaining the happy life.

> *Happy is anyone who is not offended because of me.*
>
> —Jesus' bonus Beatitude.

"Offended" in our vernacular is most often associated with insensitive and politically incorrect language. In Jesus' world, it was another one of those culturally rich words from the prophets and psalter.

Travel in the first century involved walking many miles in

open-toe sandals across unpaved, unmanaged, and uneven stony terrain. Toes were frequently stubbed on these stones, leading to a tumble and fall or a blustering curse. The Greeks had a word for these uneven stones and for people who intentionally placed these stones along the way: *skandalon.*

Skandalon, the word from which we derive our words for scan and scandal, was also trappers' jargon for tripping up (*scandalizing*) their prey.

Unapologetically, Jesus repeatedly refers to himself as a divine stumbling stone (*skandalon*). Jesus quotes from the Psalter when he says that he is, "the stone that the builders rejected," a "stone of stumbling and a rock of offense (*skandalon*)." Stumbling over Jesus apparently is a real thing. The Pharisees are tripped up by his bending of the rules. The wealthy are tripped up like a camel over his humbling Kingdom ethic. His home village of Nazareth stumbles over the moniker son-of-a-carpenter. All his disciples stumble because of the cursed nature of a Messiah on a cross. The Greco-Roman world stumbled over the foolishness of a King on a Cross.

In short, stumbling meant a failure of faith. And when we lose faith, our happy heart takes a tumble.

Faith, like toes in toeless sandals, can be a sensitive and vulnerable thing. Gouged or stubbed faith can bring down our whole being, happy heart, and all. So, it makes sense when Jesus says, "Happy is the one who does not stumble because of me."

For every nine people who get offended, there is one who doesn't. At the point of our suffering, there is a split in the road where we get to choose the way forward. Some of the happiest people are those who just don't get offended, and rather allow their faith to be refined by disappointments and suffering. Conversely, some of the most unhappy and miserable people are jaded by disappointments, lose faith in the waiting, and become bitter because of suffering.

Common Skandalon

The three stumbling stones of disappointments, delay, and unfulfilled expectations are often stones of serendipity when we continue forward in faith.

Perhaps few of us can understand the kind of disappointments and even frustration toward God that Eric Liddell, the Scottish athlete, *could* have felt. What if we had trained for years and dreamed of an Olympic gold, but were told a couple of months before the event that our religious beliefs would keep us out of the race? How would we feel about God, our faith practices, and the disruptions of our dreams? Many of us would abandon our religious convictions or become offended at God. The years of training, social sacrifices, and national expectations that come with an Olympic dream is something very few of us know.

At the ripe young age of fifteen, Liddell was heralded by his fellow Scots as the great Scot hope for representation in the Olympics one day. His rare speed, agility, and sheer athleticism were celebrated around the nation. By the time he was twenty-two, he had won Britain's 100 yard and 220-yard races, setting records in the former that would take over twenty-three years to break. He was highly favored and expected to win gold in the 100-meter race for Britain at the 1924 Olympics.

Liddell, born in China to Christian missionary parents, grew up in England at boarding schools from the time he was five years old. His personal faith grew stronger throughout boarding school and on into college. He was a sought-after communicator travelling around Scotland sharing his faith.

A couple of months before the Olympics, Liddell received the disappointing news that his preferred event, the 100-meter race, was scheduled on a Sunday. In a surprising plot twist, Liddell informed the Olympic committee that he would withdraw from his favored 100-meter race for religious reasons.

Although those who knew him were never shocked by his faith commitment, friends and family pointed out after his death that his Olympic gold aspirations and representing Scotland were a distant second to his lifelong passion of representing Christ in China. Eric said, "I believe that God made me for a purpose. But He also made me fast, and when I run, I feel His pleasure." His family pointed out how his face was always skyward, his mouth wide open, and his arms awkwardly flinging about as if he was grasping at God when he ran.

The unfazed Liddell then signed up for the Olympics 400-meter race since it wasn't on a Sunday. His record time in the event was a modest time; there really wasn't any expectation that he would medal, but he would be able to run. Unluckily, he drew the outside position on the track, which put him at another disadvantage since he wouldn't know the pace to set. The gun blasted and Liddell threw himself into the run, head back, mouth open, face looking up to God. That day Eric won the gold and set an Olympic record. He walked off the racing track and onto the mission field.

For the next eighteen years, he served as a teacher in China. In the 2008 Olympics, China honored him for abdicating his freedom in a Japanese internment camp so a pregnant woman could be free. He died in the camp shortly thereafter. One of the prisoners in the camp said of Eric, "He was Jesus in running shoes." Another imprisoned missionary said, "He was the most joyful Christian I have ever known."

How do we, like Eric, overcome the unhappiness of a disappointing turn of events? How do we remain unoffended at God when our faith practices seemingly disqualify us from our dreams? Where do we get the kind of resilient faith that takes stumbling stones in stride?

First Steps to Unoffendability

We, like Peter, may be quick to say, "We'll never stumble or be offended at you, Lord." But Peter and, for that matter, Paul, were offended by Jesus, at some point along the way. And yet, they both overcame the affronts to their faith and recovered an unoffendable joy. Let's learn from them.

The first step involves rethinking (*metanoia*) the stumbling stone. We need an expanded vision of the stumbling stone's providential possibilities. Peter and Paul both stumbled over Jesus' cross, it was, on the cultural surface, a meaningless scandal and an affront to their religious dignity. But when they saw the redemptive light of the cross, it became the reality that transformed them. Instead of a stumbling block the cross became the salvific steppingstone for their lives. Unoffendability means we have taken a step from seeing the offense as something that is *against us to* seeing the offense as something *for us.*

Peter and Paul allowed their ideas of God to expand. When God pushed the boundaries of their divine concepts of him, they chose not to sulk in a small imagination but opted for an expanded consciousness. They chose to trust in God's inherent goodness even when they could not understand. Offense usually comes from a small idea of God and a self-centric vision of life.

Both Peter and Paul fell, and when they did their preconceived ideas about God fell too, and from that fallen posture they experienced a scandalous love that unveiled itself in an unimaginable epiphany of truth.

The steps to unoffendable joy simply put are these:

1. Reframe the stumbling stone into a steppingstone by coming to trust the goodness of God.
2. Expand your ideas of God.
3. Expand your limitations of life. Let life be something that moves beyond the realms of time to realize there is more, so much more.

The Happy Dance

Hebrews eleven rattles off a list of forty heroes and heroines of faith that reads more like a poem than prose.

The Grave-Talker
The Wind-Charioteer
The Storm-Rider
The Dream-Snatcher
The One-Man Abolitionist
The Prophetess-Warrior
The Giant Slayer
The Lion-Whisperer
Three Fire-Walkers
A Whale-Rider
The Scarlet-corded Earthquake Dancer

The list abruptly halts in blunt truth: these exemplars authenticated their faith not because they received their promise, but because they didn't receive their promise! They trusted through disappointments, delayed promises, and were unoffendable. They happily trusted God for the sake of God.

If you read between-the-lines, you will know all of them stumbled their way into a dance. They flailed and fell, half-ran and half-crumbled into the arms of God, and then just went with it, made a dance move out of it and let God carry the day.

We turn the page and immediately notice that they are now crowded around the heavens watching us laugh as we, too, stumble into God.

As we approach the end, you may be hoping for us to package the book up nicely with a bow. But we want to offer you more than some cliched Hollywood ending. What if we told you that disappointments, delays, and unfulfilled expectations were *the* pathways into divine happiness? What if, as scandalous as it sounds, we need to stumble and falter into joy? What if we are interrupted into the realities that bring God near? And what if our unanswered questions are the stuff that joyful faith is made up of? The happy mystery and holy awe wait for us in inexplicable faith. After all, isn't that Jesus' way?

Consider Jesus' unoffendability. Jesus was not offended at the humble beginnings of a feeding trough bassinet. He never stumbled over his dishonorable discharge from Nazareth. His critics never made him critical. His houselessness never made him homeless. He welcomed a cross-carrying life, and even saw the cross not as God's curse on him, but as his honor to the Father! Nothing tainted his conviction that he was God's beloved son. Not the rejection of his teachings. Not dying penniless. Not the betrayal or abandonment of the Twelve. Nothing, absolutely nothing, robbed him of the joyous voice from heaven saying, "This is my Beloved Son. In him I take great joy." Jesus possessed unoffendable joy. He trusted that there was more, much more, than could be answered in some cute apologetic. He let the Father answer. And the Father answered by raising him up. Life without the resurrection would have been a hapless historical footnote. But from the other side of the cross, he says, "This is the way to unoffendable joy."

Can you trust there is much more to the stumbling stone than meets the eye? Can you believe in the goodness of God in the badness of life? This is the secret to unoffendable joy.

An Unoffendable Guillotine

John's best years were behind him, his greatest days were over. He now languishes half-forgotten in prison. There is no exit strategy, no escape from his fate, no succession plan. Jesus knows John will never see the Jordan again or preach another sermon; he knows that the only choice John has is whether he will be offended or unoffended.

The greatest prophet of all time has one more valuable lesson to teach all of us: it's not whether we question or not, but to whom we direct our questions that determines the fate of happiness. John, rightly, directs his questions to Jesus. He doesn't cast a cloud of doubt over Jesus among his disciples; neither does he announce another Messiah candidate. He takes his questions to Jesus. And what he gets in return is a reminder that the miracles of God cannot be taken hostage by imprisoning the greatest prophet of all time.[93]

Jesus answers John's question by reminding him to look at the Kingdom of God and not get distracted by the workings of men. The response the Baptist's disciples return with will not change the imprisonment of John or resolve his confusion regarding Jesus's unconventional methodology.

The joyful path never requires answers to our questions, only unoffendable faith. Evidently, these words were enough for John, his disciples never return with a need for further clarification. Shortly thereafter, the music played, the sensual Salome danced, the lustful Herod swooned, and the offended Heroditas demanded the head of John the Baptist.

John, unoffended, could lay his head down on the guillotine and rest.

✿ Trust

Trusting God feels wildly freeing. When we finally let go of the need for control and the pressure to manipulate the outcomes, there is a weightlessness and an accompanying "aha" moment that all is well, happiness is working itself out not by our effort and control but by letting it happen through God's grace to us. The joy at this discovery is freeing and empowering. Our hearts feel free, alive and living as all things are meant to live—boldly and authentically.

❖ My Happy Declaration

If a prophet, as great as John the Baptist, was offended, then I may be tempted toward offense as well. I understand that offense is a trap that robs me of my happiness. I reject offense! When I find myself tempted with offense, I will expand my vision of God. I will accept the grace of God to forgive and turn the stumbling stone into a stepping stone. I choose to trust in the goodness of God.

CHAPTER 13

BACK TO THE MOUNTAIN

Where The Resurrection Lives

> *The resurrection isn't just a surprise happy ending for one person; it is instead the turning point for everything else. It is the point at which all the old promises come true at last.*
>
> —N.T. Wright

As we bring our book to a close, it is fitting we conclude with Matthew's unique reflection on the Resurrection.

The book of Matthew begins and ends on the happy Mount of Beatitudes. Within these twenty-three between-the-mountains chapters, Jesus embodies his happy attitudes. We see his joyful lifestyle and poverty of spirit, we come to understand what it means to converse meekly, practice miracles and compassion, and mercifully forgive. Even his parables, those timeless stories, instruct us on the art of peacemaking. By the time we turn the page to his horrific crucifixion, all eight happy attitudes are in full, glorious display. We are just stumped by what seems to be a cruel, unrewarded end.

Within twenty-four hours, he is arrested, tried, sentenced, flogged, crucified and buried. What could be happy about his disciples abandoning him in the night or his mother witnessing his execution in broad daylight? Before the sun sets, his body is wrapped and sealed in a tomb. Nothing in this story ends happily. How could fear and sorrow end a life of a Man who taught love, forgiveness, and happiness?

But if we paid attention closely, we might have seen markers pointing toward the realization that Divine happiness comes through human sorrow. Three days after his burial, joy erupts through the angel's declaration, re-routing the course of Jesus' disciples. Encountering the two Marys at Jesus' tomb, the angel tells them, "He is not here, for he has risen . . . go quickly and tell his disciples that . . . *he is going before you to Galilee*" (28:7). Interestingly, in the book of Matthew, the disciples' encounter with the Resurrection doesn't happen in Judea (like Luke) or Jerusalem (like John), but Galilee.

Why Galilee? And more precisely, where in Galilee could they expect to see him? Galilee was a large province. Josephus, the first century Jewish historian, claimed there were three million people and over two hundred villages and cities. Jesus and His disciples had spent a considerable amount of time in Galilee, so how would they know where to find the resurrected Messiah?

Matthew guides us to the resurrection encounter site with these words: "Now the eleven disciples went to Galilee, *to the mountain to which Jesus had directed them.* And when they saw him, they worshiped him..." (28:16). Without careful attention, it's easy to read the story as Jesus outside his tomb, directing them to go to the mountain *specifically,* but this is not at all what Jesus said. They were simply instructed by the angel to *go to Galilee. They* decided to go to Mount of Beatitudes, where *it all began,* to the place they first heard Jesus' big idea worth sharing.

Matthew is communicating something to us about the resurrection of Jesus. According to theologian John Shea, Matthew brings his audience back to the mountain, because Jesus is resurrected in the Beatitudes. For Matthew and his readers, the focus of the resurrection was not a garden tomb, but a happy mountain—that is, as we live out the happy attitudes, the whole world comes alive with the resurrected Jesus. This new playground and landscape are where we happily live.

In our Brief History of Happiness, we discussed how

makarios was not only a serious topic among philosophers but among the common people. Yet, if you recall, this did not mean *makarios* belonged to everyone: only the privileged class were worthy of it.

Jesus directly rejected this notion. Real happiness, according to Jesus, was for everyone who followed God. So, he taught a large crowd of people from various social classes and cultural backgrounds. When we, all of us, from every walk of life, are living out these happy oracles, we can be confident in Jesus' promise,

I am with you always, to the end of the age.

These are the final words in the Book of Matthew. The resurrected Jesus speaks this to the remaining eleven disciples on the mountain. It is important to examine this affirmation in its context, to realize the significance of this verse. Before this line, Jesus instructs the eleven disciples to "make disciples of all the nations." Essentially, "go make happy people, teach them to follow me into happiness." And his happy beatitudes, because they are meant for everyone, radically challenged the idea of *makarios* of the time period.

Early followers of Jesus eventually began using the *makarios* language of Jesus to describe God. Paul in a letter to a young pastor says, "I have been entrusted with the Gospel of the *makarios* God" (1 Timothy 1:11). Again, as he signs off on the letter he says, "Makarios and only Sovereign, the King of kings and Lord of lords." (1 Timothy 6:15). As we know, *makarios* translates to happy, a true, pure, and "real" happiness. As we quoted in the beginning of this book, "We must confess that God is happiness itself" (Boethius). God is a happy God.

AFTERWORD
APOCALYPTIC BLISS

> *For men are made for happiness, and anyone who is completely happy has a right to say to himself, 'I am doing God's will on earth.' All the righteous, all the saints, all the holy martyrs were happy.*
>
> —Dostoyevsky

As part of our research for a future project, we (Mike and Jeffrey), traveled to the Greek island of Patmos where John wrote the book of Revelation. As we stepped off the ferry, an old-world charm breezed through the port city. The narrow cobblestone streets magically refracted the prisms of the New Jerusalem and filtered it through Patmian voices and faces. Sun-bleached joy whitewashed the walls. The mysterious cloud of witnesses could be detected as the Aegean winds whistled through the narrow corridors and tiny windows. Immediately, the days slowed, matching the pace of sailboats and church bells. A parliament of Little Owls outside our villa signaled the arrival of evening wisdom vespers. Over the course of several days, we studied, prayed in the Cave of the Apocalypse, and quieted our spirits in Saint John's castle-like monastery.

Our conversations, as if tugged by the spirit of Revelation, returned to Real Happy; there seemed to be one more closing word. Over coffee and Greek pastries, we retraced the steps of Real Happy and how it showed God really cares about our happiness, so much so that Jesus spelled out a clear and surprising path with eight happy oracles. These eight oracles are not a one stop shop, God wanted us to experience them as often as we can, and meditate on them as we live them out daily.

One evening from a Jerusalem-facing balcony, Mike peered out over the Aegean Sea and wrote the happy declarations that close each of the chapters you've now read. These declarations are empowering and can change everything from our moods to our spirits. We encourage you to post them and revisit these words again and again.

Mid-trip, Jeffrey spoke at the Cave of the Apocalypse on the theology of caves—Moses' Cave, David's Cave, Elijah's Cave, and John's Cave. Afterwards, he sat outside the cave reading the book of Revelation when he came across these closing words, "happy are those . . . who enter the city by the gate."[94] This verse raised the question, "Was this God's final word on happiness?"

The book of Revelation is God's final word on everything from prayer, Scripture, politics, evil, the church, and judgment.[95] John's signature mark for this final word on something was to group it into sevens. Sleuthing one's way through all the sevens and symbols of Revelation can be exciting and illuminating. There are the seven churches, the seven-headed political beast, the seven-hill city, seven secret thunders, seven seals, and seven prayers. Back at the villa, we researched the final word on happiness and happily discovered a total of seven *makarisms*[96] tucked away in Revelation!

1. "Happy is the one who reads aloud the words of this prophecy, and happy are those who hear it and take to heart what is written in it . . . ." (1:3)
2. ". . . happy are the dead who die in the Lord from now on.' 'Yes,' says the Spirit, 'they will rest from their labor, for their deeds will follow them.'" (14:13)
3. ". . . Happy is the one who stays awake and remains clothed, so as not to go naked and be shamefully exposed." (16:15)
4. "Happy are those who are invited to the wedding supper of the Lamb!'" (19:9)

5. “Happy and holy are those who share in the first resurrection.” (20:6)
6. “Happy is the one who keeps the words of the prophecy of this book.” (22:7)
7. “Happy are those who wash their robes so that they may have the right to the tree of life and may go through the gates into the city.” (22:14)

Excited and energized by this final word for Real Happy, we sensed its prophetic tone for all those who made it this far in the book.

The seven *makarisms* declare that God has the last word on happiness and mean the happiness God offers is full and complete. These seven happy prophecies merit their own book, something to which we will return in the future. We felt it fitting, however, to close this book by saying that your happy journey is destined for full and complete apocalyptic happiness (and once again, these are two words you don’t hear together).

This is the Bible’s way of saying, “and God and God’s children lived happily ever after.”

❖ My Final Declaration

I began my journey not knowing for sure how serious God was about my personal happiness. Now that I know it means so much to God, I will live my life following the path of total overflowing joy! My tears over the inevitable challenges that will come will be brief, my celebrations will be full, and my life will be happy. This is the way I pledge to live because I know that God wants it that way.

FREE RESOURCES

We have included a free happiness and spirituality toolbox at www.imrealhappy.com. The toolbox which will be dripped out over the course of the first six months will include:

1. Nine Happy Attitudes Table with Definitions (printout version)
2. Happy Declaration (printout version)
3. The Nine Happy Emotions and Descriptions
4. Making Room Assessment Tool
5. Theology of Kenosis and the Art of Self-Emptying.
6. Ashrei—The Real Happy Prayer—a weeklong devotional in happy praying.
7. Description Tool on the Quadrants of Socio-Spiritual Righteousness
8. Forgiveness FAQ
9. Theology of *skandalon* and how Jesus' scandal frees us from our scandalous regrets.
10. Art Reflection on Caravaggio's Seven Works of Mercy.
11. Comprehensive List of the Makarisms of Jesus
12. 100 Favorite Quotes on Happy Spirituality

Coming Soon: Real Happy is meant to make us aware and get us going down the path of happiness. Soon we will release both a workbook and children's book.

Workbook: think and work through Jesus' ideas on happiness (personal and group study)

Children's Book: guide your children through Jesus' path to a real happy life.

ENDNOTES

1 The quote is lifted from a larger dialogue in which Augustine is arguing that God's desire for people is to be happy. '"Does it seem to you," I said, "that God is eternal and ever abiding?" "Of course He is," Licentius said. "This is so certain that there's no need for an inquiry." All the others agreed with pious devotion. "Then he who has God," I said, "is happy." When they joyfully and most gladly accepted this, I said: "Then I imagine that we should now be seeking nothing else but who out of all men has God; for surely, he will be happy. I seek to learn your opinion about him." Here Licentius said, "He has God who lives well." Trygetius said, "He has God who does what God wants done."' Saint Augustine, *On the Happy Life (29-30).*

2 "Euthydemus" Plato. Plato Complete Works. Titan Read.

3 Darrin M. McMahon, *Happiness: A History* (39).

4 Matthew 5:3-11.

5 The New Testament was originally written in Greek, the most common written language of the Greco-Roman world. In the next chapter we will give a brief history of *makarios.*

6 In John 10:10, Jesus offers his radical life-giving joy with, "I came that they may have life and have it abundantly."

7 The Greeks had adequate words that mean blessed (*eulogotos,* from which we get our word eulogy) Matthew could have used. In fact, blessed (*eulogotos*) is used again and again in the Christian Scriptures (e.g. Luke 1:68, Ephesians 1:3). A similar choice plays out in the Hebrew Scriptures with the word happy. Hebrew has the wonderful word *baruch* (blessed) and is used to translate events like Jacob's blessing of Joseph (Genesis 48:15-16). Hebrew also has a word for happy, *ashrei,* that David, in Psalm 84:4-5, uses. In Judaism its even called the Happy Prayer. So why, if happiness is one of the greatest longings of humanity, is the word happy so frequently translated in the English Bible as blessed?

8 *Beatitudo,* the Latin word for happy, translated from the Greek word, *makarios* was coined by Cicero several centuries before Christ in his works on the Happy Life. Seneca the Younger, composes his dialogue *Beata de Vita,* "On the Happy Life" and Saint Augustine writes his dialogue *Vita de Beata,* "On the Happy Life." Jerome three centuries after Jesus will use *beatitudo* in his Latin translation of

the Bible to talk about Jesus' Happy Life promises, the Beatitudes. Another Greek word that gets translated as happy is *eudaemon*, which comes from the Greek word *eu*, meaning good and *daemon* which means spirit. When philosophers used this word they were conveying the idea that the good or virtuous life was the happy life.

9 We have laid out the literary backdrop and setting using a quote from Matthew 5:1-3 (NIV), followed by a placeholder [Sermon on the Mount], which takes up three chapters (5-7), followed by a quote from Matthew 7:28 (NIV) which reframes the closing context of the Sermon on the Mount.

10 The Happy Attitudes which are found in Matthew 5, are immediately preceded by Jesus calling four disciples—Peter, Andrew, James and John (Matthew 4:18-22). Matthew, the evangelist who writes the Gospel of Matthew, isn't called until chapter nine and the Twelve aren't appointed until chapter ten. What we are suggesting is that Jesus begins with something as innocuous as a small group of four, but by the end of the Masterclass Matthew would have us know that a contagion of joy disrupted the hillside.

11 Harvard professors Robert Waldinger and Marc Shultz, *The Good Life: Lessons from the World's Longest Scientific Study of Happiness*, disclose the findings of Harvard's eighty-four-year longitudinal study on happiness. This book identified community and relationships as the only consistent reality of happiness in the lives of the longest scientific study on happiness!

12 Jesus was more than the archetypical king, he was also the Logos and sage, which "taught them" indicates. The Wisdom Teaching was a stream of Jewish practice on the "happy" life. This is traced in the Psalms, Proverbs, and the other Ketuvim books (Wisdom Writings in the Hebrew Bible). In the next chapter, we will point out Jesus' link to these books and their teachings in his happy life sayings.

13 See Matthew 5:13-16, where Jesus completes his thoughts on the happy attitudes by saying the whole world will come to experience heaven on earth through those who live out these happy attitudes, like a little salt flavors the whole meal, a little light colors the whole world, and a city on a hill sticks out on the whole landscape.

14 *Kavanah* is the Hebrew word for intentionality. The rabbis taught that on Yom Kippur, the Torah required that the people hear the blowing of the shofar. This meant listening with intention, listening *for it* and not just to it. When compounded with *shema* (Hebrew

word for 'hear') the notion was to listen with a desire to obey. Were they *listening for it* when it blew or were they preoccupied and simply alarmed by it? To listen *for it* meant the present was focused on anticipation and that the hearer was readied for the appropriate response of worship. To hear it after it sounded meant that one would be alarmed and react out of an unprepared posture.

15 Waldinger and Shultz, *The Good Life.*

16 Matthew 26:14-16. "Then one of the twelve, whose name was Judas Iscariot, went to the chief priests and said, 'What will you give me if I deliver him over to you?' And they paid him thirty pieces of silver. And from that moment he sought an opportunity to betray him."

17 Matthew 27:3-5. It's interesting that Matthew, who records these happy sayings also gives the most detail about Judas selling Jesus for thirty pieces of silver and killing himself.

18 Rodney Stark (*Triumph of Christianity*) dispels the myth of Christianity being a movement of only poor and impoverished people by pointing to how wealthy politicians, small business owners, members of Caesar's family and Herod's court, wealthy merchants, land magnates, and several tax collectors, (to name a few) identified and devoted themselves to Christ, both before his resurrection and after. Some scholars believe that Jesus funded much of his own ministry early on and that Paul (2 Corinthians 8:9) may indicate that he came from a wealthy family, "he was rich, yet for your sake he became poor, so that you by his poverty might become rich." E. A. Judge (*The Social Pattern of Christian Groups in the First Century*) pointed out through Paul's letters how over 40 different "persons of substance, members of a cultivated social elite" were devoted to Jesus and the mission of the church. Stark concludes, "...early Christians were not a bunch of miserable underdogs. This always should have been obvious, not only from reading the Gospels, but from asking why and how a bunch of illiterate ignoramuses came to produce sophisticated written scriptures."

19 Confessions, Saint Augustine. Chapter 38.

20 This is our paraphrase from the story Jesus told in Luke 18:9-14.

21 That upper class had four groups: the Rulers, which were people like Herod and Caesar, who controlled and accessed almost half of the gross national product. The governing class—nobles, family members, and officials received almost a quarter of the gross national product. These two upper classes controlled 50-75% of the

gross national product. The lower class made up about 80% of the population and had four groups as well.

Those in this lower class were referred to as poor, but with the Greek word *penés*. They were poor because they lived hand to mouth, working whatever manual labor they could find. The first group of *penés* was the Peasants. We typically think of Peasants as being the poorest of the poor, but that was not the case in ancient agrarian societies. They're the farmers, they're the ones with a little piece of land, or as was the case in Jesus' day, many were simply tenant farmers. In many cases two-thirds (2/3) of their product went to taxes, tolls, and rents. They constitute about 60% of ancient agrarian society.

Below the peasants, surprisingly, are the artisans, the bricklayers and the carpenters. The artisans who had to work with their hands did not have a plot of land that they could use to support themselves. They depended on a patron, a benefactor to favor them with work.

Below the artisans are the Unclean, the people whose lack of skill and resources is such that they are left with the jobs that no one else wants to do—pig farmers, undertakers, trash collectors, and all minorities. The last class of people in this eight-tiered system was the Destitute (*ptōchoi*), making up 5-10% of all the lower class. The second Greek word for poor, *ptōchoi*, referred to the very bottom class of people

22 The three Jewish spiritual disciplines Jesus references can be read in Matthew 6:1-18.

23 Makarisms are happy sayings. In Acts 20:35, Paul reminds us of a *makarism* that is not included in any of the written Gospels but was part of the oral tradition. "In all things I have shown you that by working hard in this way we must help the weak and remember the words of the Lord Jesus, how he himself said, 'It is more [happy] to give than to receive.'"

24 Research has demonstrated that money can buy happiness on the condition that it is given away . One study on the relationship between generosity and happiness illustrated giving is more rewarding than keeping or spending on yourself. Michael Norton, Professor of Business Administration, Harvard, in a TED talk called "How to Buy Happiness" demonstrated with study after study how giving away money and possessions results again and again in deeper happiness. He concluded the talk by saying, "Spending on other

people has a bigger return for you than spending on yourself. If you think money cannot buy happiness it's because you are not spending it right. Stop thinking about what to buy for yourself and think of giving it away instead."

25 People who regularly worship, pray and meditate report higher levels of happiness and joy than those who don't. Several TED Talks document the power of meditation and prayer to bring about well-being and joyfulness. Professor Olga Louchakova in her article *The Essence of the Prayer of the Heart* documents cases of people healed of mental illness and psychological trauma through the Jesus' Prayer, an ancient form of contemplative prayer used by Eastern Orthodox Christian churches.

26 Study after study continues to astound professionals on the healing power of fasting on moods, mental clarity and wellbeing. A study by Andreas Michalsen in University of Berlin showed that fasting alleviates symptoms of depression and improves anxiety scores in 80% of chronic pain patients after just a few days. People often report that fasting improves moods, alertness and gives way to feelings of tranquility. In the documentary *The Science of Fasting*, a USC research project done in tandem with two other European Universities documented countless twenty-one day, water only fasts, and the emotional, mental, and even physical healing that occurred.

27 St. Bernardine of Siena said about Francis' happiness, 'When he pronounced the word 'Jesus' or heard someone say it, he was filled with joy and he seemed to be completely transformed, as if he had suddenly tasted something marvelous or caught the strain of a beautiful harmony.'

28 John 2:6, "Now there were six stone water jars there for the Jewish rites of purification, each holding twenty or thirty gallons."

29 This is a personal prayer inspired by Psalm 139.

30 *Meister Eckhart's Living Wisdom: Indestructible Joy and the Path of Letting Go* (Section 14). This was an audio reflection by James Finley, a spiritual director and clinical psychologist.

31 In the 1980's Dr. Robert Pluthik came up with the original framework of eight primary emotions which included anger, fear, sadness, disgust, surprise, anticipation, trust and joy. The University of Glasgow categorizes the human emotions into four distinct emotions. Psychologists and researchers like Brene Brown, *Maps of*

the Heart, differentiates eighty-seven different emotions. And the Junto Institute Emotion wheel has 108.

32 We have in mind here C.S. Lewis' use of the German word *Sehnsucht* (from *The Weight of Glory*), that sense of deep, inconsolable longing, yearning, the feeling of intensely missing something when we don't even know what it is. It's the longing for a home that we have never been to before. This mournful longing that Saint Augustine calls a restlessness we never overcome until we find our rest in God.

33 Psalm 1 begins with "Happy (Hebrew, *ashrei*) is the one who . . . delights himself in the instructions of the Lord." The Ashrei Prayer or Happy Prayer is prayed in Judaism at least three times a day, its called such because the prayer begins with the word happy.

34 The Babylonian Talmud completed 500 C.E. promises life in the "age to come" to those who pray the Happy Prayer three times a day.

35 We selected Robert Alter's highly acclaimed translation of the Psalms. The homespun language of "happy the folk" captures well the Jewish notion of communal happiness that happens when we walk through sorrow together.

36 Psalm 137 artistically captures this with the image of unplayed harps vacated on poplars and captives refusing to sing songs of merriment.

37 In his book, *From Strength to Strength,* Harvard Professor Arthur C. Brooks, suggests that Beethoven's deafness brought with it the gift of artistic freedom.

38 The addition of "Ode to Joy" to the final movement of Beethoven's Ninth Symphony (also known as the "Choral" movement) occurred in 1824, when Beethoven premiered the symphony in Vienna, Austria. The lyrics were adapted from "Ode to Joy", a poem written by Friedrich Schiller, by which Beethoven was deeply inspired. The inclusion of the chorus was groundbreaking, as it marked the first time that a composer had incorporated a choral section into a symphony. This represents Ode to Joy's lyrical adaptation for Beethoven's Ninth Symphony, in an English translation.

39 Without exception God is present with the afflicted. God comforts, redeems, renews, and takes up their cause. Psalm 9, 10 and 72 are just a couple examples of God's heart toward the afflicted.

40 God's heart is to be restored to his children. Even the journey that begins in mournful regret can end in tearful gratitude. Hosea 12:4 expresses this notion, "[Jacob] wept and sought [God's] favor."

David in Psalms 32, 38, and 51 gives us a sneak peek into the King's regrets and tearful spirit. Luke 7:38-46 describes the sobs from a harlot washing Jesus' feet as love and gratitude for forgiveness to which Jesus affirms, "Your faith has saved you; go in peace." The restoration is seen in that God becomes Jacob's blessing. God becomes David's honor. God becomes the harlot's peace. God comforts our repentance with his nearness and nature. The tears of tormenting spiritual loss find their happy recovery in the presence of God.

41 B.B. Warfield, *The Emotional Life of Our Lord*, studied every emotion of Jesus and concluded that compassion was the emotion that motivated his life and mission.

42 Douglas Abrams, Desmond Tutu and the Dalai Lama, *The Book of Joy*.

43 Psalms 9, 10, 35, 37, 58, 72, 82, and 94 cry out to God to judge the oppressors and make the world right. It's interesting as we walk through this list that David is both a taker and one taken from. This is frequently the case. His prayers reflect the brokenness in the world and the longing for God to make both the world and the petitioner right.

44 Remember how Jesus' "happy life" motif comes from a stream of Jewish thought called the Way of Wisdom. Many Psalms, Proverbs, and other writings were part of this single voice concerned with the good life. This wisdom tradition covered the full spectrum of the happy life, even touching on the challenges and threats to it.

45 Lecture on the Beatitudes taught to Regent College in Vancouver.

46 The gofundme page is still here: https://www.gofundme.com/f/refugee-work-in-bangkok with the amount of money Jed raised in two weeks. I asked Jed to rewrite it for Angels and Beasts (content on spiritual formation and identity-development). The moment was a defining moment for Jed, eighteen months later he tattooed Matthew 6:33 on his right bicep as a personal life-motto.

47 Waldinger and Shultz, *The Good Life (30).*

48 For years the food industry thought the way to make people happy was simply to ask them, "What do you like?" Ragu and Prego conducted focus groups for thirty years asking people how they liked their spaghetti sauce and walked away with the same results year after year. Twenty-seven percent of the people in the focus groups would claim they bought it because they really liked it and the

others bought it because it's all they knew. Harvard psychophysicist, Howard Moskowitz, took a different approach to getting to people's likes and dislikes. He created forty-five different flavors and did tastings, giving them an opportunity to discover what they really liked. He discovered that thirty-three percent of the people loved extra chunky sauce. Another thirty percent preferred spicy. Over the course of thirty years of focus groups no one ever said they liked it extra chunky, even though a third of them, deep down, had appetites for a chunkier sauce. Over the next ten years chunky sauce grossed $600 million alone.

Moskowitz discovered that people don't know what they like; they have to be shown what they like. Moskowitz's breakthrough with spaghetti sauce changed the food industry. Before his study there was only one kind of sauce. Today Ragu sells over twenty varieties of sauces. And this breakthrough continued into coffee, beverages, fast foods, and on and on.

Acclaimed journalist Malcolm Gladwell gave a TED talk on happiness where he claimed Howard Moskowitz did "as much to make Americans happy as perhaps anyone over the last 20 years." Gladwell put it like this: critical to understanding our quest for happiness is to "realize that we cannot always explain what we want deep down." We need someone to come along and show us what our heart has an appetite for.

49 Clark Pinnock in *A Wideness to God's Mercy* argues that the mercy of God is for the whole world (John 3:16); a mercy that is wider than one religion, race, gender, etc. A mercy as ubiquitous as the air—available to animals, plants, people. Right above our nose and under our nose, in our nose. James Finley, *The Healing Path,* describes his encounter with mercy: "One day as I walked back and forth in the loft of the barn reading the Psalms, I began to realize that what we tend to think of as the air is actually God. In a subtle, interior way I sensed that I was walking back and forth in the atmospheric, all-encompassing presence of God, who was sustaining me breath by breath. I can recall realizing that if I were to try to flee from the atmospheric, all-encompassing presence of God that, no matter where I would flee to, God would be sustaining me in my flight from God, and that wherever my arrival point might be, God would be waiting for me when I got there."

50 Psalm 136.

51 Helen Luke in *Old Age* shares the exchange insight on mercy and then says, "the root meaning of exchange persisted and developed in another context, its meaning deepening through the French merci to grateful response and kindness of heart, and finally to the compassion and forgiveness, including all our share of darkness, whereby we are able to open ourselves to the Mercy. This is the ultimate 'exchange' that, when we come to a final letting go, may reveal to us the whole."

52 Jesus offers us two parables to demonstrate the exchange of mercy, the Parable of the Merciless Servant (Matthew 18:21-35) and the Good Samaritan (Luke 10:25-37). Both parables use money to reinforce how mercy exacts a cost. The first parable talks about the cost of mercy in the context of forgiveness (releasing another from their indebtedness to us and bearing the debt within ourselves). The second parable talks about the cost of mercy in the context of compassion (paying for the care, healing and restoration of another who was wronged by others). What Jesus has in mind when he blesses the merciful, that is those full of mercy, is both these trajectories of mercy: forgiveness and compassion.

53 The first sign of turning water into wine (John 2:1-12) is immediately followed by the cleansing of the Temple (John 2:13-22).

54 Gordon-Conwell Theological Seminary doctoral research project by Dr. Jeffrey Garner, *Reflections on the Spiritual Intimacy of the Pastor using the Beloved Disciple as a Rubric.*

55 Thomas Merton in his book *The Sign of Jonas* speaks of an epiphany of mercy that he is given as God speaks to him that God is mercy, within mercy, within mercy.

56 Author Jonathan Aitken estimates this figure in *John Newton: From Disgrace to Amazing Grace.*

57 Fyodor Dostoevsky, *The Brothers Karamazov.*

58 B. B. Warfield, one of the great Princeton theologians, did a study on the emotional life of Jesus and noted how the Gospels used "moved with compassion" more frequently than any other term to describe Jesus's emotional life. He pointed out that mercy was a word unknown to the Greek classics but was likely a Greek word coined by Jews to describe the Divine feeling of pity and tender mercy.

Abraham Heschel's comparative observation of the major gods noted that the god of the philosophers was too sublime to possess a heart, the pagan gods had animal passions, but the God of Israel had passion and his prophets portrayed a passion full of mercy, compassion, and justice, this is something no other god possessed. Thus to feel compassion was to feel the intense feeling of God's mercy.

Jesus was deeply in touch with his emotional side and possessed the ability to be touched by the plight of others. What he did with that—healing the sick, raising the dead, feeding the hungry, bringing words of comfort and hope—was the outward work.

59 Douglas Abrams records this conversation of the Dalai Lama in his book *The Book of Joy.*

60 Abraham Joshua Heschel, a Jewish philosopher and theologian, emphasized God's compassion as the basis for Jewish ethics and social justice, and is expressed in the Jewish concept of *tikkun olam* (the repair of the world). See also, Rabbi Harold Kushner, Rabbi Joseph Telushkin, Rabbi Shai Held. Christian theologians who emphasized compassion as central to the emotion of God include: Walter Brueggemann, B. B. Warfield, Henri Nouwen, Thomas Oord, Ilia Delio, and Miroslav Volf.

61 "Why do your disciples break the tradition of the elders? For they do not wash their hands when they eat" (Matthew 15:2).

62 Darrin M. McMahon, *Happiness: A History* (65).

63 Lewis, C. S. *The Problem of Pain* (p. 95). HarperCollins. Kindle Edition.

64 *Summa Theologica* (Complete & Unabridged) (p. 1578). Coyote Canyon Press. Kindle Edition.

65 We are grateful for Eugene Peterson's lecture on the Beatitudes from Regent College in Vancouver. Peterson compares the two mountains of Beatitudes and Sinai pointing out the beauty of Sinai and how the Beatitudes continued that beautiful moment and wasn't a critique of it.

66 "He is the image of the invisible God, the firstborn of all creation." (Colossians 1:15)

67 Psalm 24:4-6 (emphasis added).

68 Davis, Gerald J. *The Divine Comedy: The New Translation by Gerald J. Davis.* Insignia Publishing. Kindle Edition. (the last line of the Divine Comedy).

69 Gerald Davis' *New Translation of The Divine Comedy,* Canto XXVII.

70 Lewis, C. S. *Till We Have Faces* (p. 335). HarperCollins. Kindle Edition.

[71] We could see how C. S. Lewis' *Till We Have Faces* would fit as a mythology for "the pure in heart shall see God." The layers of meaning and profundity are a worthy exploration for those who feel especially drawn to this beatitude.

[72] Sermon 57, page 298. *The Complete Mystical Works of Meister Eckhart.* Translated and edited by Maurice O'C. Walshe. Revised with a Foreword by Bernard McGinn. A Herder & Herder Book. The Crossroad Publishing Company, New York

[73] Darrin McMahon, *Happiness: A History* (2), lays out the fascinating history of happiness and all of its fits and turns and how ugly its outcomes were early on.

[74] A November 2020 study done by the University College London found loneliness to be the number one cause for depression in older adults. This is just one of many studies with similar findings. Mother Teresa famously said, "The most terrible poverty is loneliness, and the feeling of being unloved."

[75] Nelson Mandela's book *Long Walk to Freedom: The Autobiography of Nelson Mandela* takes the reader on a transformational journey of peace as Mandela shows his own inner journey with peace resulted in the external mission of being a peacemaker.

[76] In Paul's instruction on the Eucharist (1 Corinthians 11:17-34), he says, "Everyone ought to examine themselves before they eat of the bread and drink from the cup. For those who eat and drink without discerning the body of Christ eat and drink judgment on themselves." (vss. 28-29). The examination Paul is calling his readers to engage in is discerning the body of Christ and making sure they are at peace with each other and that there is no discrimination, prejudice, or cliques.

[77] Richard Rohr, *The Wisdom Pattern,* (50).

[78] Desmond Tutu and Mpho Tutu, *The Book of Forgiving: The Fourfold Path for Healing Ourselves and Our World.*

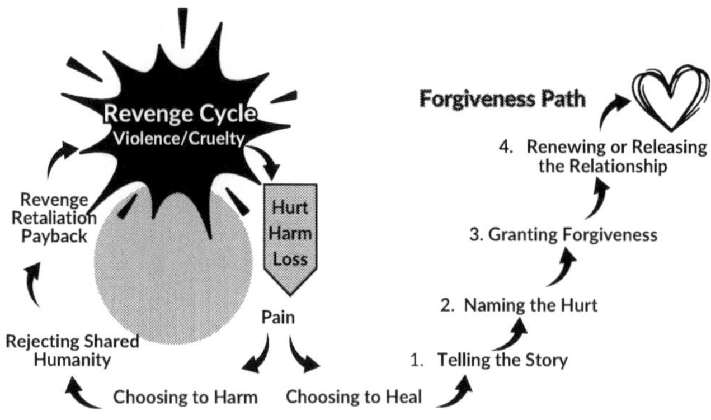

This image is adapted from Tutu and Tutu's book.

79 John 20:20-21 (NIV).

80 Johannine Scholar, Sandra Schneiders, in her book *Jesus Risen in Our Midst,* takes chapter 5 to talk about what it means to forgive. She argues that our mission is to continue the mission that Jesus began of forgiving sins. Not only was forgiveness central to Jesus' ministry, but it is the continuing ministry the Spirit comes upon us to achieve.

81 Boethius. *The Consolation of Philosophy* (18). Translated by Søren Filipski.

82 Douglas Abrams was shocked by the volume of questions along these lines of happiness and suffering. He devotes a whole chapter to the subject in his book with the Dalai Lama and Desmond Tutu, *The Book of Joy.*

83 Darrin McMahon, *Happiness: A History* (81).

84 We are thinking here of Richard Rohr's life mandate, "The best criticism of the bad is the practice of the better." He talks about this in his book *Eager to Love: The Alternative Way of Francis of Assisi* (42).

85 Dietrich Bonhoeffer, *The Cost of Discipleship* (113).

86 Desmond Tutu said, "You know, when Nelson Mandela went to jail, he was young and, you could almost say, bloodthirsty. He was head of the armed wing of the African National Congress, his party. He spent twenty-seven years in jail, and many would say, Twenty-seven years, oh, what a waste. And I think people are surprised when I say no, the twenty-seven years were necessary. They were necessary to

remove the dross. The suffering in prison helped him to become more magnanimous, willing to listen to the other side. To discover that the people he regarded as his enemy, they too were human beings who had fears and expectations. And they had been molded by their society. And so without the twenty-seven years I don't think we would have seen the Nelson Mandela with the compassion, the magnanimity, the capacity to put himself in the shoes of the other." *The Book of Joy* (43).

87 This quote is often misattributed to Abraham Lincoln, but it's more likely an anonymous quote.

88 *The Book of Joy* (47).

89 Darrin McMahon, *Happiness: A History* (95).

90 Acts 6:15.

91 Due to being born when his parents were very old, he was likely raised by the Essene orphanage out in the wilderness. His Scriptural mission of "voice of one crying in the wilderness" (Matthew 3:3) and his minimalist life of "locusts and wild honey" (v. 4) are Essene signatures. His frequent fasting, demand for people to assemble in the wilderness and be baptized as opposed to the ritual baths at Herod's Temple, his denouncement of social injustices and inequality, and rebuke of the Herod Antipas adulterous life all point to the fact that he was most likely affiliated with the Essenes.

92 Jesus doesn't answer this question. The question of whether he is the One is for us to answer, not Jesus. This question is something we must sort out with God and can only come to it by faith.

93 Luke reports, "In that hour he healed many people of diseases and plagues and evil spirits, and on many who were blind he bestowed sight. And he answered them, 'Go and tell John what you have seen and heard: the blind receive their sight, the lame walk, lepers are cleansed, and the deaf hear, the dead are raised up, the poor have good news preached to them. And blessed is the one who is not offended by me.'" (7:21-23).

94 Revelation 22:14 (Jeffrey Garner's personal translation).

95 Eugene Petersen, *Reversed Thunder,* approaches the Book of Revelation as a prayer book which sees worship as the final word placed in the Canon of Scripture.

ABOUT THE BOOK

When almost every human choice is made with happiness in mind, why do we continue to miss out on lasting happiness? Perhaps happiness isn't something we pursue but rather something that ensues...What if happiness is not stuff we fill up on but something we make room for? Real happiness may not be something out there at all (material 🚗+🏠) but something in here (spiritual ♡).

In this compelling narrative, best-selling author Mike Hayes and Dr. Jeffrey Garner journey through the eight beloved Beatitudes from Jesus' revolutionary Sermon on the Mount. Religious and non-religious readers alike will smile and feel inspired in learning that Jesus, despite popular understandings, was in fact deeply invested in human happiness. Jesus' happiness, however, consoles sorrow, embraces emptiness, confronts injustice, and is even present in our suffering—all that we avoid in our search for happiness. Aptly reframing the Beatitudes as happy oracles, Mike and Jeffrey share personal stories and historical insights that optimize Jesus' happy message for a 21st century audience. This book challenges our cultural conceptions of happiness and beautifully guides the reader into Jesus' Real Happy life.